CHARACTERISTICS OF A GREAT
CHRIST-CENTERED
MARRIAGE

Copyright

© 2025 Lord & Benoit Publishing

ISBN: 978-0-9888692-8-8

The Bible is not copywritten, but the translations are. Each publisher/translator extends gratis permission to use their *translation* of the Bible when less than 500/1000 verses from each translation are quoted. Links to detailed rights for each translator/publisher are below. This book complies with all publisher requirements.

Scripture quotations marked (AMPC) were taken from the Amplified® Bible, Copyright © 1954, 1958, 1962, 1964, 1965, 1987 by The Lockman Foundation. Used by permission. All rights reserved, www.lockman.org" https://www.lockman.org/permission-to-quote-copyright-trademark-information/

Scripture quotations marked (NASB1995) were from the New American Standard Bible®, Copyright © 1960, 1971, 1977, 1995 by The Lockman Foundation. Used by permission. All rights reserved. www.lockman.org" https://www.lockman.org/permission-to-quote-copyright-trademark-information/

Scripture marked (NKJV) were from the New King James Version®. Copyright © 1982 by Thomas Nelson. Used by permission. All rights reserved.
https://www.thomasnelson.com/about-us/permissions/#permissionBiblequote

Scripture quotations marked (ESV) are from the ESV® Bible (The Holy Bible, English Standard Version®), copyright © 2001 by Crossway, a publishing ministry of Good News Publishers. Used by permission. All rights reserved."
https://www.crossway.org/permissions/

Scripture marked (WEB) were from the World English Bible. The name "World English Bible" is trademarked. The World English Bible is a no copyright Modern English translation of the Holy Bible. The World English Bible is based on the American Standard Version of the Holy Bible first published in 1901, the Biblia Hebraica Stutgartensa Old Testament, and the Greek Majority Text New Testament. For more information, please see the World English Bible Frequently Asked Questions and the legal and status page at https://ebible.org/eng-web/copyright.htm

Acknowledgements

Lead Contributor: B Benoit

Prayer Support: L Benoit

Prioritization Contributor(s): A Bese, D Bese

Cover Illustrator: A Bese

Cover Photo: Christian Engagement Picture by Bible verses 70

Contents

Biblical Foundation of Marriage 1
- #1   Ephesians 5:25-33 (NASB1995) 1
- #2   Colossians 3:12-17 (NKJV) 2
- #3   Proverbs 18:16-24 (NKJV) 3
- #4   Matthew 19:1-12 (WEB) 4
- #5   Psalm 127 (WEB) 6

Controlling the Tongue 7
- #6   Philippians 2:14-18 (WEB) 7
- #7   James 3 (WEB) 8
- #8   Matthew 7:1-12 (NKJV) 10
- #9   Romans 14:13-26 (WEB) 12
- #10   James 4 (ESV) 14
- #11   Romans 12:1-9 (AMPC) 16
- #12   Colossians 3:1-11 (NKJV) 19

Agape Love 20
- #13   1 Corinthians 13:1-14:1 (ESV) 20
- #14   1 John 4:1-12 (WEB) 22
- #15   Philippians 1:27-2:4 (NKJV) 24
- #16   Philippians 2:1-13 (WEB) 26
- #17   1 Peter 4:1-11 (NASB1995) 28
- #18   John 13:28-38 (WEB) 30

Commitment and Trust 32
- #19   2 Timothy 2:15-26 (WEB) 32
- #20   Malachi 2 (NASB1995) 34
- #21   Galatians 5:13-18 (ESV) 36

| #22 | Jeremiah 17:5-10 (NKJV) | 37 |
| #23 | James 5:13-20 (WEB) | 38 |

Respect 39

#24	Proverbs 15:1-10 (ESV)	39
#25	Colossians 3:18-4:6 (NKJV)	40
#26	Romans 12:10-21 (AMPC)	42
#27	1 Peter 3:1-7 (NKJV)	44
#28	James 1:19-26 (NASB1995)	45
#29	Proverbs 31:10-31 (WEB)	46

Prayer and Worship 48

#30	1 Thessalonians 5:8-28 (WEB)	48
#31	Philippians 4:1-13 (WEB)	50
#32	Matthew 18:15-20 (WEB)	52
#33	Ephesians 6:16-24 (ESV)	53
#34	Psalm 34:1-10 (NKJV)	54
#35	Joshua 24:14-18 (NKJV)	55

Faith and Spiritual Growth 56

#36	James 1:1-11 (NASB1995)	56
#37	Hebrews 11:1-13 (NKJV)	58
#38	Hebrews 10:19-31 (WEB)	60
#39	Galatians 6:1-10 (WEB)	62

Communication and Forgiveness 63

#40	Ephesians 4:25-32 (WEB)	63
#41	Matthew 6:9-21 (WEB)	64
#42	Mark 11:22-33 (AMPC)	66
#43	Luke 17:1-10 (WEB)	68

#44	Matthew 18:21-35 (WEB)	70

Patience and Appreciating One Another 72

#45	Ephesians 3:14-4:7 (WEB)	72
#46	Ephesians 4:1-16 (WEB)	74
#47	Ecclesiastes 4 (AMPC)	76
#48	Ephesians 5:15-24 (WEB)	78
#49	Galatians 5:18-26 (NKJV)	79

Work/Life Balance 80

#50	1 Corinthians 6:9-20 (ESV)	80
#51	1 Timothy 6:17-21 (WEB)	82
#52	Matthew 26:36-41 (WEB)	83
#53	Ephesians 5:1-13 (WEB)	84
#54	1 Corinthians 10:1-13 (WEB)	86
#55	1 Peter 5:8-14 (WEB)	88

Investing in Your Children 89

#56	Ephesians 6:1-9 (WEB)	89
#57	Proverbs 22:1-16 (WEB)	90
#58	Deuteronomy 6:1-9 (WEB)	92
#59	Colossians 3:18-4:6 (NKJV)	94

Joy and Hope for the Future 96

#60	Proverbs 17:16-28 (WEB)	96
#61	Romans 15:1-13 (WEB)	98
#62	Philippians 1:1-14 (WEB)	100
#63	Romans 8:24-34 (NASB1995)	102
#64	Psalm 16 (NKJV)	104

Appendix A – Instructor Guide for Interactive Bible Learning 105

The Good News about Jesus Christ 109

Biblical Foundation of Marriage
#1 Ephesians 5:25-33 (NASB1995)

Husbands, love your wives, just as Christ also loved the church and gave Himself up for her, [26] so that He might sanctify her, having cleansed her by the washing of water with the word, [27] that He might present to Himself the church [a]in all her glory, having no spot or wrinkle or any such thing; but that she would be holy and blameless. [28] So husbands ought also to love their own wives as their own bodies. He who loves his own wife loves himself; [29] for no one ever hated his own flesh, but nourishes and cherishes it, just as Christ also *does* the church, [30] because we are members of His body. [31] For this reason a man shall leave his father and mother and shall be joined to his wife, and the two shall become one flesh. [32] This mystery is great; but I am speaking with reference to Christ and the church. [33] Nevertheless, each individual among you also is to love his own wife even as himself, and the wife must *see to it* that she [b]respects her husband.

What insight does God give us in this Scripture about the characteristics of a Christ-centered marriage?

What distractions are noted in this text that might tempt someone to not embrace characteristics of a Christ-centered marriage?

Take a minute and ask the Lord how He wants you to apply this Scripture to your life going forward (and we'll go around the room)?

#2 Colossians 3:12-17 (NKJV)

Therefore, as *the* elect of God, holy and beloved, put on tender mercies, kindness, humility, meekness, longsuffering; [13] bearing with one another, and forgiving one another, if anyone has a complaint against another; even as Christ forgave you, so you also *must do*. [14] But above all these things put on love, which is the bond of perfection. [15] And let the peace of God rule in your hearts, to which also you were called in one body; and be thankful. [16] Let the word of Christ dwell in you richly in all wisdom, teaching and admonishing one another in psalms and hymns and spiritual songs, singing with grace in your hearts to the Lord. [17] And whatever you do in word or deed, *do* all in the name of the Lord Jesus, giving thanks to God the Father through Him.

What insight does God give us in this Scripture about the characteristics of a Christ-centered marriage?

What distractions are noted in this text that might tempt someone to not embrace characteristics of a Christ-centered marriage?

Take a minute and ask the Lord how He wants you to apply this Scripture to your life going forward (and we'll go around the room)?

#3 Proverbs 18:16-24 (NKJV)

A man's gift makes room for him, and brings him before great men. [17] The first *one* to plead his cause *seems* right, until his neighbor comes and examines him. [18] Casting lots causes contentions to cease, and keeps the mighty apart. [19] A brother offended *is harder to win* than a strong city, and contentions *are* like the bars of a castle. [20] A man's stomach shall be satisfied from the fruit of his mouth; *from* the produce of his lips he shall be filled. [21] Death and life *are* in the power of the tongue, and those who love it will eat its fruit. [22] *He who* finds a wife finds a good *thing,* and obtains favor from the Lord. [23] The poor *man* uses entreaties, but the rich answers roughly. [24] A man *who has* friends must himself be friendly, but there is a friend *who* sticks closer than a brother.

What insight does God give us in this Scripture about the characteristics of a Christ-centered marriage?

What distractions are noted in this text that might tempt someone to not embrace characteristics of a Christ-centered marriage?

Take a minute and ask the Lord how He wants you to apply this Scripture to your life going forward (and we'll go around the room)?

#4 Matthew 19:1-12 (WEB)

When Jesus had finished these words, he departed from Galilee and came into the borders of Judea beyond the Jordan. ² Great multitudes followed him, and he healed them there. ³ Pharisees came to him, testing him and saying, "Is it lawful for a man to divorce his wife for any reason?" ⁴ He answered, "Haven't you read that he who made them from the beginning made them male and female, Genesis 1:27 ⁵ and said, 'For this cause a man shall leave his father and mother, and shall be joined to his wife; and the two shall become one flesh?' Genesis 2:24 ⁶ So that they are no more two, but one flesh. What therefore God has joined together, don't let man tear apart." ⁷ They asked him, "Why then did Moses command us to give her a certificate of divorce and divorce her?" ⁸ He said to them, "Moses, because of the hardness of your hearts, allowed you to divorce your wives, but from the beginning it has not been so. ⁹ I tell you that whoever divorces his wife, except for sexual immorality, and marries another, commits adultery; and he who marries her when she is divorced commits adultery." ¹⁰ His disciples said to him, "If this is the case of the man with his wife, it is not expedient to marry." ¹¹ But he said to them, "Not all men can receive this saying, but those to whom it is given. ¹² For there are eunuchs who were born that way from their mother's womb, and there are eunuchs who were made eunuchs by men; and there are eunuchs who made themselves eunuchs for the Kingdom of Heaven's sake. He who is able to receive it, let him receive it."

What insight does God give us in this Scripture about the characteristics of a Christ-centered marriage?

What distractions are noted in this text that might tempt someone to not embrace characteristics of a Christ-centered marriage?

Take a minute and ask the Lord how He wants you to apply this Scripture to your life going forward (and we'll go around the room)?

#5 Psalm 127 (WEB)

Unless Yahweh builds the house,
   they who build it labor in vain.
Unless Yahweh watches over the city,
   the watchman guards it in vain.
² It is vain for you to rise up early,
   to stay up late,
   eating the bread of toil,
   for he gives sleep to his loved ones.
³ Behold, children are a heritage of Yahweh.
   The fruit of the womb is his reward.
⁴ As arrows in the hand of a mighty man,
   so are the children of youth.
⁵ Happy is the man who has his quiver full of them.
   They won't be disappointed when they speak with their enemies in the gate.

What insight does God give us in this Scripture about the characteristics of a Christ-centered marriage?

What distractions are noted in this text that might tempt someone to not embrace characteristics of a Christ-centered marriage?

Take a minute and ask the Lord how He wants you to apply this Scripture to your life going forward (and we'll go around the room)?

Controlling the Tongue
#6 Philippians 2:14-18 (WEB)

Do all things without complaining and arguing, ¹⁵ that you may become blameless and harmless, children of God without defect in the middle of a crooked and perverse generation, among whom you are seen as lights in the world, ¹⁶ holding up the word of life, that I may have something to boast in the day of Christ, that I didn't run in vain nor labor in vain. ¹⁷ Yes, and if I am poured out on the sacrifice and service of your faith, I rejoice, and rejoice with you all. ¹⁸ In the same way, you also rejoice, and rejoice with me.

What insight does God give us in this Scripture about the characteristics of a Christ-centered marriage?

What distractions are noted in this text that might tempt someone to not embrace characteristics of a Christ-centered marriage?

Take a minute and ask the Lord how He wants you to apply this Scripture to your life going forward (and we'll go around the room)?

#7 James 3 ^(WEB)

Let not many of you be teachers, my brothers, knowing that we will receive heavier judgment. ²For we all stumble in many things. Anyone who doesn't stumble in word is a perfect person, able to bridle the whole body also. ³Indeed, we put bits into the horses' mouths so that they may obey us, and we guide their whole body. ⁴Behold, the ships also, though they are so big and are driven by fierce winds, are yet guided by a very small rudder, wherever the pilot desires. ⁵So the tongue is also a little member, and boasts great things. See how a small fire can spread to a large forest! ⁶And the tongue is a fire. The world of iniquity among our members is the tongue, which defiles the whole body, and sets on fire the course of nature, and is set on fire by Gehenna. ⁷For every kind of animal, bird, creeping thing, and sea creature, is tamed, and has been tamed by mankind; ⁸but nobody can tame the tongue. It is a restless evil, full of deadly poison. ⁹With it we bless our God and Father, and with it we curse men who are made in the image of God. ¹⁰Out of the same mouth comes blessing and cursing. My brothers, these things ought not to be so. ¹¹Does a spring send out from the same opening fresh and bitter water? ¹²Can a fig tree, my brothers, yield olives, or a vine figs? Thus no spring yields both salt water and fresh water. ¹³Who is wise and understanding among you? Let him show by his good conduct that his deeds are done in gentleness of wisdom. ¹⁴But if you have bitter jealousy and selfish ambition in your heart, don't boast and don't lie against the truth. ¹⁵This wisdom is not that which comes down from above, but is earthly, sensual, and demonic. ¹⁶For where jealousy and selfish ambition are, there is confusion and every evil deed. ¹⁷But the wisdom that is from above is first pure, then peaceful, gentle, reasonable, full of mercy and good fruits, without partiality, and without hypocrisy. ¹⁸Now the fruit of righteousness is sown in peace by those who make peace.

What insight does God give us in this Scripture about the characteristics of a Christ-centered marriage?

What distractions are noted in this text that might tempt someone to not embrace characteristics of a Christ-centered marriage?

Take a minute and ask the Lord how He wants you to apply this Scripture to your life going forward (and we'll go around the room)?

#8 Matthew 7:1-12 (NKJV)

"Don't judge, so that you won't be judged. ²For with whatever judgment you judge, you will be judged; and with whatever measure you measure, it will be measured to you. ³Why do you see the speck that is in your brother's eye, but don't consider the beam that is in your own eye? ⁴Or how will you tell your brother, 'Let me remove the speck from your eye,' and behold, the beam is in your own eye? ⁵You hypocrite! First remove the beam out of your own eye, and then you can see clearly to remove the speck out of your brother's eye. ⁶"Don't give that which is holy to the dogs, neither throw your pearls before the pigs, lest perhaps they trample them under their feet, and turn and tear you to pieces. ⁷"Ask, and it will be given you. Seek, and you will find. Knock, and it will be opened for you. ⁸For everyone who asks receives. He who seeks finds. To him who knocks it will be opened. ⁹Or who is there among you who, if his son asks him for bread, will give him a stone? ¹⁰Or if he asks for a fish, who will give him a serpent? ¹¹If you then, being evil, know how to give good gifts to your children, how much more will your Father who is in heaven give good things to those who ask him! ¹²Therefore, whatever you desire for men to do to you, you shall also do to them; for this is the law and the prophets.

What insight does God give us in this Scripture about the characteristics of a Christ-centered marriage?

What distractions are noted in this text that might tempt someone to not embrace characteristics of a Christ-centered marriage?

Take a minute and ask the Lord how He wants you to apply this Scripture to your life going forward (and we'll go around the room)?

#9 Romans 14:13-26 (WEB)

Therefore let's not judge one another any more, but judge this rather, that no man put a stumbling block in his brother's way, or an occasion for falling. [14] I know, and am persuaded in the Lord Jesus, that nothing is unclean of itself; except that to him who considers anything to be unclean, to him it is unclean. [15] Yet if because of food your brother is grieved, you walk no longer in love. Don't destroy with your food him for whom Christ died. [16] Then don't let your good be slandered, [17] for God's Kingdom is not eating and drinking, but righteousness, peace, and joy in the Holy Spirit. [18] For he who serves Christ in these things is acceptable to God and approved by men. [19] So then, let's follow after things which make for peace, and things by which we may build one another up. [20] Don't overthrow God's work for food's sake. All things indeed are clean, however it is evil for that man who creates a stumbling block by eating. [21] It is good to not eat meat, drink wine, nor do anything by which your brother stumbles, is offended, or is made weak. [22] Do you have faith? Have it to yourself before God. Happy is he who doesn't judge himself in that which he approves. [23] But he who doubts is condemned if he eats, because it isn't of faith; and whatever is not of faith is sin. [24] Now to him who is able to establish you according to my Good News and the preaching of Jesus Christ, according to the revelation of the mystery which has been kept secret through long ages, [25] but now is revealed, and by the Scriptures of the prophets, according to the commandment of the eternal God, is made known for obedience of faith to all the nations; [26] to the only wise God, through Jesus Christ, to whom be the glory forever! Amen.

What insight does God give us in this Scripture about the characteristics of a Christ-centered marriage?

What distractions are noted in this text that might tempt someone to not embrace characteristics of a Christ-centered marriage?

Take a minute and ask the Lord how He wants you to apply this Scripture to your life going forward (and we'll go around the room)?

#10 James 4 (ESV)

What causes quarrels and what causes fights among you? Is it not this, that your passions are at war within you? ² You desire and do not have, so you murder. You covet and cannot obtain, so you fight and quarrel. You do not have, because you do not ask. ³ You ask and do not receive, because you ask wrongly, to spend it on your passions. ⁴ You adulterous people! Do you not know that friendship with the world is enmity with God? Therefore whoever wishes to be a friend of the world makes himself an enemy of God. ⁵ Or do you suppose it is to no purpose that the Scripture says, "He yearns jealously over the spirit that he has made to dwell in us"? ⁶ But he gives more grace. Therefore it says, "God opposes the proud but gives grace to the humble." ⁷ Submit yourselves therefore to God. Resist the devil, and he will flee from you. ⁸ Draw near to God, and he will draw near to you. Cleanse your hands, you sinners, and purify your hearts, you double-minded. ⁹ Be wretched and mourn and weep. Let your laughter be turned to mourning and your joy to gloom. ¹⁰ Humble yourselves before the Lord, and he will exalt you. ¹¹ Do not speak evil against one another, brothers. The one who speaks against a brother or judges his brother, speaks evil against the law and judges the law. But if you judge the law, you are not a doer of the law but a judge. ¹² There is only one lawgiver and judge, he who is able to save and to destroy. But who are you to judge your neighbor? ¹³ Come now, you who say, "Today or tomorrow we will go into such and such a town and spend a year there and trade and make a profit"— ¹⁴ yet you do not know what tomorrow will bring. What is your life? For you are a mist that appears for a little time and then vanishes. ¹⁵ Instead you ought to say, "If the Lord wills, we will live and do this or that." ¹⁶ As it is, you boast in your arrogance. All such boasting is evil. ¹⁷ So whoever knows the right thing to do and fails to do it, for him it is sin.

Characteristics of a Great Christ-Centered Marriage

What insight does God give us in this Scripture about the characteristics of a Christ-centered marriage?

What distractions are noted in this text that might tempt someone to not embrace characteristics of a Christ-centered marriage?

Take a minute and ask the Lord how He wants you to apply this Scripture to your life going forward (and we'll go around the room)?

#11   Romans 12:1-9 (AMPC)

I appeal to you therefore, brethren, *and* beg of you in view of [all] the mercies of God, to make a decisive dedication of your bodies [presenting all your members and faculties] as a living sacrifice, holy (devoted, consecrated) and well pleasing to God, which is your reasonable (rational, intelligent) service *and* spiritual worship. ²Do not be conformed to this world (this age), [fashioned after and adapted to its external, superficial customs], but be transformed (changed) by the [entire] renewal of your mind [by its new ideals and its new attitude], so that you may prove [for yourselves] what is the good and acceptable and perfect will of God, *even* the thing which is good and acceptable and perfect [in His sight for you]. ³For by the grace (unmerited favor of God) given to me I warn everyone among you not to estimate *and* think of himself more highly than he ought [not to have an exaggerated opinion of his own importance], but to rate his ability with sober judgment, each according to the degree of faith apportioned by God to him. ⁴For as in one physical body we have many parts (organs, members) and all of these parts do not have the same function *or* use, ⁵So we, numerous as we are, are one body in Christ (the Messiah) and individually we are parts one of another [mutually dependent on one another]. ⁶Having gifts (faculties, talents, qualities) that differ according to the grace given us, let us use them: [He whose gift is] prophecy, [let him prophesy] according to the proportion of his faith; ⁷[He whose gift is] practical service, let him give himself to serving; he who teaches, to his teaching; ⁸He who exhorts (encourages), to his exhortation; he who contributes, let him do it in simplicity *and* liberality; he who gives aid *and* superintends, with zeal *and* singleness of mind; he who does acts of mercy, with genuine cheerfulness *and* joyful eagerness. ⁹[Let your] love be sincere (a real thing); hate what is evil [loathe all ungodliness, turn in horror from wickedness], but hold fast to that which is good.

What insight does God give us in this Scripture about the characteristics of a Christ-centered marriage?

What distractions are noted in this text that might tempt someone to not embrace characteristics of a Christ-centered marriage?

Take a minute and ask the Lord how He wants you to apply this Scripture to your life going forward (and we'll go around the room)?

#12   Colossians 3:1-11 ^(NKJV)

If then you were raised with Christ, seek those things which are above, where Christ is, sitting at the right hand of God. ²Set your mind on things above, not on things on the earth. ³For you died, and your life is hidden with Christ in God. ⁴When Christ *who is* our life appears, then you also will appear with Him in glory. ⁵Therefore put to death your members which are on the earth: fornication, uncleanness, passion, evil desire, and covetousness, which is idolatry. ⁶Because of these things the wrath of God is coming upon the sons of disobedience, ⁷in which you yourselves once walked when you lived in them. ⁸But now you yourselves are to put off all these: anger, wrath, malice, blasphemy, filthy language out of your mouth. ⁹Do not lie to one another, since you have put off the old man with his deeds, ¹⁰and have put on the new *man* who is renewed in knowledge according to the image of Him who created him, ¹¹where there is neither Greek nor Jew, circumcised nor uncircumcised, barbarian, Scythian, slave *nor* free, but Christ *is* all and in all.

What insight does God give us in this Scripture about the characteristics of a Christ-centered marriage?

What distractions are noted in this text that might tempt someone to not embrace characteristics of a Christ-centered marriage?

Take a minute and ask the Lord how He wants you to apply this Scripture to your life going forward (and we'll go around the room)?

Agape Love
#13   1 Corinthians 13:1-14:1 (ESV)

If I speak with the tongues of men and of angels, but do not have love, I have become a noisy gong or a clanging cymbal. ² If I have *the gift of* prophecy, and know all mysteries and all knowledge; and if I have all faith, so as to remove mountains, but do not have love, I am nothing. ³ And if I give all my possessions to feed *the poor*, and if I surrender my body to be burned, but do not have love, it profits me nothing. ⁴ Love is patient, love is kind *and* is not jealous; love does not brag *and* is not arrogant, ⁵ does not act unbecomingly; it does not seek its own, is not provoked, does not take into account a wrong *suffered*, ⁶ does not rejoice in unrighteousness, but rejoices with the truth; ⁷ bears all things, believes all things, hopes all things, endures all things. ⁸ Love never fails; but if *there are gifts of* prophecy, they will be done away; if *there are* tongues, they will cease; if *there is* knowledge, it will be done away. ⁹ For we know in part and we prophesy in part; ¹⁰ but when the perfect comes, the partial will be done away. ¹¹ When I was a child, I used to speak like a child, think like a child, reason like a child; when I became a man, I did away with childish things. ¹² For now we see in a mirror dimly, but then face to face; now I know in part, but then I will know fully just as I also have been fully known. ¹³ But now faith, hope, love, abide these three; but the greatest of these is love. ¹⁴:¹ Pursue love, yet desire earnestly spiritual *gifts*, but especially that you may prophesy.

What insight does God give us in this Scripture about the characteristics of a Christ-centered marriage?

What distractions are noted in this text that might tempt someone to not embrace characteristics of a Christ-centered marriage?

Take a minute and ask the Lord how He wants you to apply this Scripture to your life going forward (and we'll go around the room)?

#14 1 John 4:1-12 (WEB)

Beloved, don't believe every spirit, but test the spirits, whether they are of God, because many false prophets have gone out into the world. ² By this you know the Spirit of God: every spirit who confesses that Jesus Christ has come in the flesh is of God, ³ and every spirit who doesn't confess that Jesus Christ has come in the flesh is not of God, and this is the spirit of the Antichrist, of whom you have heard that it comes. Now it is in the world already. ⁴ You are of God, little children, and have overcome them; because greater is he who is in you than he who is in the world. ⁵ They are of the world. Therefore they speak of the world, and the world hears them. ⁶ We are of God. He who knows God listens to us. He who is not of God doesn't listen to us. By this we know the spirit of truth, and the spirit of error. ⁷ Beloved, let's love one another, for love is of God; and everyone who loves has been born of God, and knows God. ⁸ He who doesn't love doesn't know God, for God is love. ⁹ By this God's love was revealed in us, that God has sent his one and only Son into the world that we might live through him. ¹⁰ In this is love, not that we loved God, but that he loved us, and sent his Son as the atoning sacrifice for our sins. ¹¹ Beloved, if God loved us in this way, we also ought to love one another. ¹² No one has seen God at any time. If we love one another, God remains in us, and his love has been perfected in us.

What insight does God give us in this Scripture about the characteristics of a Christ-centered marriage?

What distractions are noted in this text that might tempt someone to not embrace characteristics of a Christ-centered marriage?

Take a minute and ask the Lord how He wants you to apply this Scripture to your life going forward (and we'll go around the room)?

#15   Philippians 1:27-2:4 (NKJV)

Only let your conduct be worthy of the gospel of Christ, so that whether I come and see you or am absent, I may hear of your affairs, that you stand fast in one spirit, with one mind striving together for the faith of the gospel, ²⁸ and not in any way terrified by your adversaries, which is to them a proof of perdition, but to you of salvation, and that from God. ²⁹ For to you it has been granted on behalf of Christ, not only to believe in Him, but also to suffer for His sake, ³⁰ having the same conflict which you saw in me and now hear *is* in me. ²:¹ Therefore if *there is* any consolation in Christ, if any comfort of love, if any fellowship of the Spirit, if any affection and mercy, ² fulfill my joy by being like-minded, having the same love, *being* of one accord, of one mind. ³ *Let* nothing *be done* through selfish ambition or conceit, but in lowliness of mind let each esteem others better than himself. ⁴ Let each of you look out not only for his own interests, but also for the interests of others.

What insight does God give us in this Scripture about the characteristics of a Christ-centered marriage?

What distractions are noted in this text that might tempt someone to not embrace characteristics of a Christ-centered marriage?

Take a minute and ask the Lord how He wants you to apply this Scripture to your life going forward (and we'll go around the room)?

#16   Philippians 2:1-13 (WEB)

If therefore there is any exhortation in Christ, if any consolation of love, if any fellowship of the Spirit, if any tender mercies and compassion, ²make my joy full by being like-minded, having the same love, being of one accord, of one mind; ³doing nothing through rivalry or through conceit, but in humility, each counting others better than himself; ⁴each of you not just looking to his own things, but each of you also to the things of others. ⁵Have this in your mind, which was also in Christ Jesus, ⁶who, existing in the form of God, didn't consider equality with God a thing to be grasped, ⁷but emptied himself, taking the form of a servant, being made in the likeness of men. ⁸And being found in human form, he humbled himself, becoming obedient to the point of death, yes, the death of the cross. ⁹Therefore God also highly exalted him, and gave to him the name which is above every name, ¹⁰that at the name of Jesus every knee should bow, of those in heaven, those on earth, and those under the earth, ¹¹and that every tongue should confess that Jesus Christ is Lord, to the glory of God the Father. ¹²So then, my beloved, even as you have always obeyed, not only in my presence, but now much more in my absence, work out your own salvation with fear and trembling. ¹³For it is God who works in you both to will and to work, for his good pleasure.

What insight does God give us in this Scripture about the characteristics of a Christ-centered marriage?

Characteristics of a Great Christ-Centered Marriage

What distractions are noted in this text that might tempt someone to not embrace characteristics of a Christ-centered marriage?

Take a minute and ask the Lord how He wants you to apply this Scripture to your life going forward (and we'll go around the room)?

#17   1 Peter 4:1-11 (NASB1995)

Therefore, since Christ has suffered in the flesh, arm yourselves also with the same purpose, because he who has suffered in the flesh has ceased from sin, ²so as to live the rest of the time in the flesh no longer for the lusts of men, but for the will of God. ³For the time already past is sufficient *for you* to have carried out the desire of the Gentiles, having pursued a course of sensuality, lusts, drunkenness, carousing, drinking parties and abominable idolatries. ⁴In *all* this, they are surprised that you do not run with *them* into the same excesses of dissipation, and they malign *you*; ⁵but they will give account to Him who is ready to judge the living and the dead. ⁶For the gospel has for this purpose been preached even to those who are dead, that though they are judged in the flesh as men, they may live in the Spirit according to *the will of* God. ⁷The end of all things is near; therefore, be of sound judgment and sober *spirit* for the purpose of prayer. ⁸Above all, keep fervent in your love for one another, because love covers a multitude of sins. ⁹Be hospitable to one another without complaint. ¹⁰As each one has received a *special* gift, employ it in serving one another as good stewards of the multifaceted grace of God. ¹¹Whoever speaks *is to do so* as *one who is speaking* actual words of God; whoever serves *is to do so* as *one who is serving* by the strength which God supplies; so that in all things God may be glorified through Jesus Christ, to whom belongs the glory and dominion forever and ever. Amen.

What insight does God give us in this Scripture about the characteristics of a Christ-centered marriage?

What distractions are noted in this text that might tempt someone to not embrace characteristics of a Christ-centered marriage?

Take a minute and ask the Lord how He wants you to apply this Scripture to your life going forward (and we'll go around the room)?

#18   John 13:28-38 (WEB)

Now nobody at the table knew why he said this to him. ²⁹ For some thought, because Judas had the money box, that Jesus said to him, "Buy what things we need for the feast," or that he should give something to the poor. ³⁰ Therefore having received that morsel, he went out immediately. It was night. ³¹ When he had gone out, Jesus said, "Now the Son of Man has been glorified, and God has been glorified in him. ³² If God has been glorified in him, God will also glorify him in himself, and he will glorify him immediately. ³³ Little children, I will be with you a little while longer. You will seek me, and as I said to the Jews, 'Where I am going, you can't come,' so now I tell you. ³⁴ A new commandment I give to you, that you love one another. Just as I have loved you, you also love one another. ³⁵ By this everyone will know that you are my disciples, if you have love for one another." ³⁶ Simon Peter said to him, "Lord, where are you going?" Jesus answered, "Where I am going, you can't follow now, but you will follow afterwards." ³⁷ Peter said to him, "Lord, why can't I follow you now? I will lay down my life for you." ³⁸ Jesus answered him, "Will you lay down your life for me? Most certainly I tell you, the rooster won't crow until you have denied me three times.

What insight does God give us in this Scripture about the characteristics of a Christ-centered marriage?

CHARACTERISTICS OF A GREAT CHRIST-CENTERED MARRIAGE

What distractions are noted in this text that might tempt someone to not embrace characteristics of a Christ-centered marriage?

Take a minute and ask the Lord how He wants you to apply this Scripture to your life going forward (and we'll go around the room)?

Commitment and Trust
#19 2 Timothy 2:15-26 (WEB)

Give diligence to present yourself approved by God, a workman who doesn't need to be ashamed, properly handling the Word of Truth. [16] But shun empty chatter, for it will go further in ungodliness, [17] and those words will consume like gangrene, of whom is Hymenaeus and Philetus: [18] men who have erred concerning the truth, saying that the resurrection is already past, and overthrowing the faith of some. [19] However God's firm foundation stands, having this seal, "The Lord knows those who are his, "Numbers 16:5 and, "Let every one who names the name of the Lord depart from unrighteousness." [20] Now in a large house there are not only vessels of gold and of silver, but also of wood and of clay. Some are for honor, and some for dishonor. [21] If anyone therefore purges himself from these, he will be a vessel for honor, sanctified, and suitable for the master's use, prepared for every good work. [22] Flee from youthful lusts; but pursue righteousness, faith, love, and peace with those who call on the Lord out of a pure heart. [23] But refuse foolish and ignorant questionings, knowing that they generate strife. [24] The Lord's servant must not quarrel, but be gentle toward all, able to teach, patient, [25] in gentleness correcting those who oppose him: perhaps God may give them repentance leading to a full knowledge of the truth, [26] and they may recover themselves out of the devil's snare, having been taken captive by him to his will.

What insight does God give us in this Scripture about the characteristics of a Christ-centered marriage?

What distractions are noted in this text that might tempt someone to not embrace characteristics of a Christ-centered marriage?

Take a minute and ask the Lord how He wants you to apply this Scripture to your life going forward (and we'll go around the room)?

#20 Malachi 2 (NASB1995)

"And now this commandment is for you, O priests. ²If you do not listen, and if you do not take it to heart to give honor to My name," says the Lord of hosts, "then I will send the curse upon you and I will curse your blessings; and indeed, I have cursed them *already*, because you are not taking *it* to heart. ³Behold, I am going to rebuke your offspring, and I will spread refuse on your faces, the refuse of your feasts; and you will be taken away with it. ⁴Then you will know that I have sent this commandment to you, that My covenant may continue with Levi," says the Lord of hosts. ⁵"My covenant with him was *one of* life and peace, and I gave them to him *as an object of* reverence; so he revered Me and stood in awe of My name. ⁶True instruction was in his mouth and unrighteousness was not found on his lips; he walked with Me in peace and uprightness, and he turned many back from iniquity. ⁷For the lips of a priest should preserve knowledge, and men should seek instruction from his mouth; for he is the messenger of the Lord of hosts. ⁸But as for you, you have turned aside from the way; you have caused many to stumble by the instruction; you have corrupted the covenant of Levi," says the Lord of hosts. ⁹"So I also have made you despised and abased before all the people, just as you are not keeping My ways but are showing partiality in the instruction. ¹⁰"Do we not all have one father? Has not one God created us? Why do we deal treacherously each against his brother so as to profane the covenant of our fathers? ¹¹Judah has dealt treacherously, and an abomination has been committed in Israel and in Jerusalem; for Judah has profaned the sanctuary of the Lord which He loves and has married the daughter of a foreign god. ¹²*As* for the man who does this, may the Lord cut off from the tents of Jacob *everyone* who awakes and answers, or who presents an offering to the Lord of hosts. ¹³"This is another thing you do: you cover the altar of the Lord with tears, with weeping and with groaning, because He no longer regards the offering or accepts *it with* favor from your hand. ¹⁴ Yet you say, 'For what reason?' Because the Lord has been a witness between you and the wife of your youth, against whom you have dealt treacherously, though she is your companion and your wife by covenant. ¹⁵ But not one has done *so* who has a remnant of the Spirit. And what did *that* one *do* while he was seeking a godly offspring? Take heed then to your spirit, and let no one deal treacherously against the wife of your youth. ¹⁶ For I hate divorce," says the Lord, the God of Israel, "and him who covers his garment with wrong," says the Lord of hosts. "So take heed to your spirit, that you do not deal treacherously." ¹⁷ You have wearied the Lord with your words. Yet you say, "How have we wearied *Him*?" In that you say, "Everyone who does evil is good in the sight of the Lord, and He delights in them," or, "Where is the God of justice?"

What insight does God give us in this Scripture about the characteristics of a Christ-centered marriage?

What distractions are noted in this text that might tempt someone to not embrace characteristics of a Christ-centered marriage?

Take a minute and ask the Lord how He wants you to apply this Scripture to your life going forward (and we'll go around the room)?

#21   Galatians 5:13-18 (ESV)

For you were called to freedom, brothers. Only do not use your freedom as an opportunity for the flesh, but through love serve one another. [14] For the whole law is fulfilled in one word: "You shall love your neighbor as yourself." [15] But if you bite and devour one another, watch out that you are not consumed by one another. [16] But I say, walk by the Spirit, and you will not gratify the desires of the flesh. [17] For the desires of the flesh are against the Spirit, and the desires of the Spirit are against the flesh, for these are opposed to each other, to keep you from doing the things you want to do. [18] But if you are led by the Spirit, you are not under the law.

What insight does God give us in this Scripture about the characteristics of a Christ-centered marriage?

What distractions are noted in this text that might tempt someone to not embrace characteristics of a Christ-centered marriage?

Take a minute and ask the Lord how He wants you to apply this Scripture to your life going forward (and we'll go around the room)?

#22   Jeremiah 17:5-10 (NKJV)

Thus says the Lord: "Cursed *is* the man who trusts in man and makes flesh his strength, whose heart departs from the Lord. [6] For he shall be like a shrub in the desert, and shall not see when good comes, but shall inhabit the parched places in the wilderness, *in* a salt land *which is* not inhabited. [7] "Blessed *is* the man who trusts in the Lord, and whose hope is the Lord. [8] For he shall be like a tree planted by the waters, which spreads out its roots by the river, and will not fear when heat comes; but its leaf will be green, and will not be anxious in the year of drought, nor will cease from yielding fruit. [9] "The heart *is* deceitful above all *things, a*nd desperately wicked; who can know it? [10] I, the Lord, search the heart, *I* test the mind, even to give every man according to his ways, according to the fruit of his doings.

What insight does God give us in this Scripture about the characteristics of a Christ-centered marriage?

What distractions are noted in this text that might tempt someone to not embrace characteristics of a Christ-centered marriage?

Take a minute and ask the Lord how He wants you to apply this Scripture to your life going forward (and we'll go around the room)?

#23 James 5:13-20 (WEB)

Is any among you suffering? Let him pray. Is any cheerful? Let him sing praises. ¹⁴ Is any among you sick? Let him call for the elders of the assembly, and let them pray over him, anointing him with oil in the name of the Lord, ¹⁵ and the prayer of faith will heal him who is sick, and the Lord will raise him up. If he has committed sins, he will be forgiven. ¹⁶ Confess your offenses to one another, and pray for one another, that you may be healed. The insistent prayer of a righteous person is powerfully effective. ¹⁷ Elijah was a man with a nature like ours, and he prayed earnestly that it might not rain, and it didn't rain on the earth for three years and six months. ¹⁸ He prayed again, and the sky gave rain, and the earth produced its fruit. ¹⁹ Brothers, if any among you wanders from the truth and someone turns him back, ²⁰ let him know that he who turns a sinner from the error of his way will save a soul from death and will cover a multitude of sins.

What insight does God give us in this Scripture about the characteristics of a Christ-centered marriage?

What distractions are noted in this text that might tempt someone to not embrace characteristics of a Christ-centered marriage?

Take a minute and ask the Lord how He wants you to apply this Scripture to your life going forward (and we'll go around the room)?

Respect
#24   Proverbs 15:1-10 ^(ESV)

A soft answer turns away wrath, but a harsh word stirs up anger. ² The tongue of the wise commends knowledge, but the mouths of fools pour out folly. ³ The eyes of the Lord are in every place, keeping watch on the evil and the good. ⁴ A gentle tongue is a tree of life, but perverseness in it breaks the spirit. ⁵ A fool despises his father's instruction, but whoever heeds reproof is prudent. ⁶ In the house of the righteous there is much treasure, but trouble befalls the income of the wicked. ⁷ The lips of the wise spread knowledge; not so the hearts of fools. ⁸ The sacrifice of the wicked is an abomination to the Lord, but the prayer of the upright is acceptable to him. ⁹ The way of the wicked is an abomination to the Lord, but he loves him who pursues righteousness. ¹⁰ There is severe discipline for him who forsakes the way; whoever hates reproof will die.

What insight does God give us in this Scripture about the characteristics of a Christ-centered marriage?

What distractions are noted in this text that might tempt someone to not embrace characteristics of a Christ-centered marriage?

Take a minute and ask the Lord how He wants you to apply this Scripture to your life going forward (and we'll go around the room)?

#25 Colossians 3:18-4:6 (NKJV)

Wives, submit to your own husbands, as is fitting in the Lord. [19] Husbands, love your wives and do not be bitter toward them. [20] Children, obey your parents in all things, for this is well pleasing to the Lord. [21] Fathers, do not provoke your children, lest they become discouraged. [22] Bondservants, obey in all things your masters according to the flesh, not with eyeservice, as men-pleasers, but in sincerity of heart, fearing God. [23] And whatever you do, do it heartily, as to the Lord and not to men, [24] knowing that from the Lord you will receive the reward of the inheritance; for you serve the Lord Christ. [25] But he who does wrong will be repaid for what he has done, and there is no partiality. [4:1] Masters, give your bondservants what is just and fair, knowing that you also have a Master in heaven. [2] Continue earnestly in prayer, being vigilant in it with thanksgiving; [3] meanwhile praying also for us, that God would open to us a door for the word, to speak the mystery of Christ, for which I am also in chains, [4] that I may make it manifest, as I ought to speak. [5] Walk in wisdom toward those *who are* outside, redeeming the time. [6] *Let* your speech always *be* with grace, seasoned with salt, that you may know how you ought to answer each one.

What insight does God give us in this Scripture about the characteristics of a Christ-centered marriage?

What distractions are noted in this text that might tempt someone to not embrace characteristics of a Christ-centered marriage?

Take a minute and ask the Lord how He wants you to apply this Scripture to your life going forward (and we'll go around the room)?

#26   Romans 12:10-21 (AMPC)

Love one another with brotherly affection [as members of one family], giving precedence *and* showing honor to one another. [11] Never lag in zeal *and* in earnest endeavor; be aglow *and* burning with the Spirit, serving the Lord. [12] Rejoice *and* exult in hope; be steadfast and patient in suffering *and* tribulation; be constant in prayer. [13] Contribute to the needs of God's people [sharing in the necessities of the saints]; pursue the practice of hospitality. [14] Bless those who persecute you [who are cruel in their attitude toward you]; bless and do not curse them. [15] Rejoice with those who rejoice [sharing others' joy], and weep with those who weep [sharing others' grief]. [16] Live in harmony with one another; do not be haughty (snobbish, high-minded, exclusive), but readily adjust yourself to [people, things] *and* give yourselves to humble tasks. Never overestimate yourself *or* be wise in your own conceits. [17] Repay no one evil for evil, but take thought for what is honest *and* proper *and* noble [aiming to be above reproach] in the sight of everyone. [18] If possible, as far as it depends on you, live at peace with everyone. [19] Beloved, never avenge yourselves, but leave the way open for [God's] wrath; for it is written, Vengeance is Mine, I will repay (requite), says the Lord. [20] But if your enemy is hungry, feed him; if he is thirsty, give him drink; for by so doing you will heap burning coals upon his head. [21] Do not let yourself be overcome by evil, but overcome (master) evil with good.

What insight does God give us in this Scripture about the characteristics of a Christ-centered marriage?

What distractions are noted in this text that might tempt someone to not embrace characteristics of a Christ-centered marriage?

Take a minute and ask the Lord how He wants you to apply this Scripture to your life going forward (and we'll go around the room)?

#27 1 Peter 3:1-7 (NKJV)

Wives, likewise, *be* submissive to your own husbands, that even if some do not obey the word, they, without a word, may be won by the conduct of their wives, ²when they observe your chaste conduct *accompanied* by fear. ³Do not let your adornment be *merely* outward—arranging the hair, wearing gold, or putting on *fine* apparel— ⁴rather *let it be* the hidden person of the heart, with the incorruptible *beauty* of a gentle and quiet spirit, which is very precious in the sight of God. ⁵For in this manner, in former times, the holy women who trusted in God also adorned themselves, being submissive to their own husbands, ⁶as Sarah obeyed Abraham, calling him lord, whose daughters you are if you do good and are not afraid with any terror. ⁷Husbands, likewise, dwell with *them* with understanding, giving honor to the wife, as to the weaker vessel, and as *being* heirs together of the grace of life, that your prayers may not be hindered.

What insight does God give us in this Scripture about the characteristics of a Christ-centered marriage?

What distractions are noted in this text that might tempt someone to not embrace characteristics of a Christ-centered marriage?

Take a minute and ask the Lord how He wants you to apply this Scripture to your life going forward (and we'll go around the room)?

#28 James 1:19-26 (NASB1995)

This you know, my beloved brethren. But everyone must be quick to hear, slow to speak *and* slow to anger; [20] for the anger of man does not achieve the righteousness of God. [21] Therefore, putting aside all filthiness and *all* that remains of wickedness, in humility receive the word implanted, which is able to save your souls. [22] But prove yourselves doers of the word, and not merely hearers who delude themselves. [23] For if anyone is a hearer of the word and not a doer, he is like a man who looks at his natural face in a mirror; [24] for *once* he has looked at himself and gone away, he has immediately forgotten what kind of person he was. [25] But one who looks intently at the perfect law, the *law* of liberty, and abides by it, not having become a forgetful hearer but an effectual doer, this man will be blessed in what he does. [26] If anyone thinks himself to be religious, and yet does not bridle his tongue but deceives his *own* heart, this man's religion is worthless.

What insight does God give us in this Scripture about the characteristics of a Christ-centered marriage?

What distractions are noted in this text that might tempt someone to not embrace characteristics of a Christ-centered marriage?

Take a minute and ask the Lord how He wants you to apply this Scripture to your life going forward (and we'll go around the room)?

#29   Proverbs 31:10-31 (WEB)

Who can find a worthy woman? For her price is far above rubies. [11] The heart of her husband trusts in her. He shall have no lack of gain. [12] She does him good, and not harm, all the days of her life. [13] She seeks wool and flax, and works eagerly with her hands. [14] She is like the merchant ships. She brings her bread from afar. [15] She rises also while it is yet night, gives food to her household, and portions for her servant girls. [16] She considers a field, and buys it. With the fruit of her hands, she plants a vineyard. [17] She arms her waist with strength, and makes her arms strong. [18] She perceives that her merchandise is profitable. Her lamp doesn't go out by night.

[19] She lays her hands to the distaff, and her hands hold the spindle. [20] She opens her arms to the poor; yes, she extends her hands to the needy. [21] She is not afraid of the snow for her household; for all her household are clothed with scarlet. [22] She makes for herself carpets of tapestry. Her clothing is fine linen and purple. [23] Her husband is respected in the gates, when he sits among the elders of the land. [24] She makes linen garments and sells them, and delivers sashes to the merchant. [25] Strength and dignity are her clothing. She laughs at the time to come. [26] She opens her mouth with wisdom. Kind instruction is on her tongue. [27] She looks well to the ways of her household, and doesn't eat the bread of idleness. [28] Her children rise up and call her blessed. Her husband also praises her: [29] "Many women do noble things, but you excel them all." [30] Charm is deceitful, and beauty is vain; but a woman who fears Yahweh, she shall be praised. [31] Give her of the fruit of her hands! Let her works praise her in the gates!

What insight does God give us in this Scripture about the characteristics of a Christ-centered marriage?

What distractions are noted in this text that might tempt someone to not embrace characteristics of a Christ-centered marriage?

Take a minute and ask the Lord how He wants you to apply this Scripture to your life going forward (and we'll go around the room)?

Prayer and Worship

#30 1 Thessalonians 5:8-28 (WEB)

But since we belong to the day, let's be sober, putting on the breastplate of faith and love, and for a helmet, the hope of salvation. [9] For God didn't appoint us to wrath, but to the obtaining of salvation through our Lord Jesus Christ, [10] who died for us, that, whether we wake or sleep, we should live together with him. [11] Therefore exhort one another, and build each other up, even as you also do. [12] But we beg you, brothers, to know those who labor among you, and are over you in the Lord, and admonish you, [13] and to respect and honor them in love for their work's sake. Be at peace among yourselves. [14] We exhort you, brothers: Admonish the disorderly; encourage the faint-hearted; support the weak; be patient toward all. [15] See that no one returns evil for evil to anyone, but always follow after that which is good for one another and for all. [16] Always rejoice. [17] Pray without ceasing. [18] In everything give thanks, for this is the will of God in Christ Jesus toward you. [19] Don't quench the Spirit. [20] Don't despise prophecies. [21] Test all things, and hold firmly that which is good. [22] Abstain from every form of evil. [23] May the God of peace himself sanctify you completely. May your whole spirit, soul, and body be preserved blameless at the coming of our Lord Jesus Christ. [24] He who calls you is faithful, who will also do it. [25] Brothers, pray for us. [26] Greet all the brothers with a holy kiss. [27] I solemnly command you by the Lord that this letter be read to all the holy brothers. [28] The grace of our Lord Jesus Christ be with you. Amen.

What insight does God give us in this Scripture about the characteristics of a Christ-centered marriage?

What distractions are noted in this text that might tempt someone to not embrace characteristics of a Christ-centered marriage?

Take a minute and ask the Lord how He wants you to apply this Scripture to your life going forward (and we'll go around the room)?

#31 Philippians 4:1-13 (WEB)

Therefore, my brothers, beloved and longed for, my joy and crown, stand firm in the Lord in this way, my beloved. [2] I exhort Euodia, and I exhort Syntyche, to think the same way in the Lord. [3] Yes, I beg you also, true partner, help these women, for they labored with me in the Good News with Clement also, and the rest of my fellow workers, whose names are in the book of life. [4] Rejoice in the Lord always! Again I will say, "Rejoice!" [5] Let your gentleness be known to all men. The Lord is at hand. [6] In nothing be anxious, but in everything, by prayer and petition with thanksgiving, let your requests be made known to God. [7] And the peace of God, which surpasses all understanding, will guard your hearts and your thoughts in Christ Jesus. [8] Finally, brothers, whatever things are true, whatever things are honorable, whatever things are just, whatever things are pure, whatever things are lovely, whatever things are of good report: if there is any virtue and if there is any praise, think about these things. [9] The things which you learned, received, heard, and saw in me: do these things, and the God of peace will be with you. [10] But I rejoice in the Lord greatly, that now at length you have revived your thought for me; in which you did indeed take thought, but you lacked opportunity. [11] Not that I speak because of lack, for I have learned in whatever state I am, to be content in it. [12] I know how to be humbled, and I also know how to abound. In everything and in all things I have learned the secret both to be filled and to be hungry, both to abound and to be in need. [13] I can do all things through Christ, who strengthens me.

What insight does God give us in this Scripture about the characteristics of a Christ-centered marriage?

What distractions are noted in this text that might tempt someone to not embrace characteristics of a Christ-centered marriage?

Take a minute and ask the Lord how He wants you to apply this Scripture to your life going forward (and we'll go around the room)?

#32   Matthew 18:15-20 (WEB)

"If your brother sins against you, go, show him his fault between you and him alone. If he listens to you, you have gained back your brother. ¹⁶ But if he doesn't listen, take one or two more with you, that at the mouth of two or three witnesses every word may be established. Deuteronomy 19:15 ¹⁷ If he refuses to listen to them, tell it to the assembly. If he refuses to hear the assembly also, let him be to you as a Gentile or a tax collector. ¹⁸ Most certainly I tell you, whatever things you bind on earth will have been bound in heaven, and whatever things you release on earth will have been released in heaven. ¹⁹ Again, assuredly I tell you, that if two of you will agree on earth concerning anything that they will ask, it will be done for them by my Father who is in heaven. ²⁰ For where two or three are gathered together in my name, there I am in the middle of them."

What insight does God give us in this Scripture about the characteristics of a Christ-centered marriage?

What distractions are noted in this text that might tempt someone to not embrace characteristics of a Christ-centered marriage?

Take a minute and ask the Lord how He wants you to apply this Scripture to your life going forward (and we'll go around the room)?

#33 Ephesians 6:16-24 (ESV)

In all circumstances take up the shield of faith, with which you can extinguish all the flaming darts of the evil one; [17] and take the helmet of salvation, and the sword of the Spirit, which is the word of God, [18] praying at all times in the Spirit, with all prayer and supplication. To that end, keep alert with all perseverance, making supplication for all the saints, [19] and also for me, that words may be given to me in opening my mouth boldly to proclaim the mystery of the gospel, [20] for which I am an ambassador in chains, that I may declare it boldly, as I ought to speak. [21] So that you also may know how I am and what I am doing, Tychicus the beloved brother and faithful minister in the Lord will tell you everything. [22] I have sent him to you for this very purpose, that you may know how we are, and that he may encourage your hearts. [23] Peace be to the brothers, and love with faith, from God the Father and the Lord Jesus Christ. [24] Grace be with all who love our Lord Jesus Christ with love incorruptible.

What insight does God give us in this Scripture about the characteristics of a Christ-centered marriage?

What distractions are noted in this text that might tempt someone to not embrace characteristics of a Christ-centered marriage?

Take a minute and ask the Lord how He wants you to apply this Scripture to your life going forward (and we'll go around the room)?

#34 Psalm 34:1-10 (NKJV)

I will bless the Lord at all times; His praise *shall* continually *be* in my mouth. ² My soul shall make its boast in the Lord; the humble shall hear *of it* and be glad. ³ Oh, magnify the Lord with me, and let us exalt His name together. ⁴ I sought the Lord, and He heard me, and delivered me from all my fears. ⁵ They looked to Him and were radiant, and their faces were not ashamed. ⁶ This poor man cried out, and the Lord heard *him, a*nd saved him out of all his troubles. ⁷ The angel of the Lord encamps all around those who fear Him, and delivers them. ⁸ Oh, taste and see that the Lord *is* good; blessed *is* the man *who* trusts in Him! ⁹ Oh, fear the Lord, you His saints! *There is* no want to those who fear Him. ¹⁰ The young lions lack and suffer hunger; but those who seek the Lord shall not lack any good *thing*.

What insight does God give us in this Scripture about the characteristics of a Christ-centered marriage?

What distractions are noted in this text that might tempt someone to not embrace characteristics of a Christ-centered marriage?

Take a minute and ask the Lord how He wants you to apply this Scripture to your life going forward (and we'll go around the room)?

#35 Joshua 24:14-18 (NKJV)

"Now therefore, fear the Lord, serve Him in sincerity and in truth, and put away the gods which your fathers served on the other side of the River and in Egypt. Serve the Lord! "Give ear, O heavens, and I will speak; and hear, O earth, the words of my mouth. [15] And if it seems evil to you to serve the Lord, choose for yourselves this day whom you will serve, whether the gods which your fathers served that *were* on the other side of the River, or the gods of the Amorites, in whose land you dwell. But as for me and my house, we will serve the Lord." [16] So the people answered and said: "Far be it from us that we should forsake the Lord to serve other gods; [17] for the Lord our God *is* He who brought us and our fathers up out of the land of Egypt, from the house of bondage, who did those great signs in our sight, and preserved us in all the way that we went and among all the people through whom we passed. [18] And the Lord drove out from before us all the people, including the Amorites who dwelt in the land. We also will serve the Lord, for He *is* our God."

What insight does God give us in this Scripture about the characteristics of a Christ-centered marriage?

What distractions are noted in this text that might tempt someone to not embrace characteristics of a Christ-centered marriage?

Take a minute and ask the Lord how He wants you to apply this Scripture to your life going forward (and we'll go around the room)?

Faith and Spiritual Growth
#36   James 1:1-11 (NASB1995)

James, a bond-servant of God and of the Lord Jesus Christ, to the twelve tribes who are dispersed abroad: Greetings. ²Consider it all joy, my brethren, when you encounter various trials, ³knowing that the testing of your faith produces endurance. ⁴And let endurance have *its* perfect result, so that you may be perfect and complete, lacking in nothing. ⁵But if any of you lacks wisdom, let him ask of God, who gives to all generously and without reproach, and it will be given to him. ⁶But he must ask in faith without any doubting, for the one who doubts is like the surf of the sea, driven and tossed by the wind. ⁷For that man ought not to expect that he will receive anything from the Lord, ⁸*being* a double-minded man, unstable in all his ways. ⁹But let the brother in humble circumstances glory in his high position; ¹⁰and the rich, in that he is made humble, because like the flower in the grass, he will pass away. ¹¹For the sun arises with the scorching wind and withers the grass, and the flower in it falls, and the beauty of its appearance perishes. So the rich man will also fade away in his pursuits.

What insight does God give us in this Scripture about the characteristics of a Christ-centered marriage?

What distractions are noted in this text that might tempt someone to not embrace characteristics of a Christ-centered marriage?

Take a minute and ask the Lord how He wants you to apply this Scripture to your life going forward (and we'll go around the room)?

#37   Hebrews 11:1-13 (NKJV)

Now faith is the substance of things hoped for, the evidence of things not seen. ²For by it the elders obtained a *good* testimony. ³By faith we understand that the worlds were framed by the word of God, so that the things which are seen were not made of things which are visible. ⁴By faith Abel offered to God a more excellent sacrifice than Cain, through which he obtained witness that he was righteous, God testifying of his gifts; and through it he being dead still speaks. ⁵By faith Enoch was taken away so that he did not see death, "and was not found, because God had taken him"; for before he was taken he had this testimony, that he pleased God. ⁶But without faith *it is* impossible to please *Him,* for he who comes to God must believe that He is, and *that* He is a rewarder of those who diligently seek Him. ⁷By faith Noah, being divinely warned of things not yet seen, moved with godly fear, prepared an ark for the saving of his household, by which he condemned the world and became heir of the righteousness which is according to faith. ⁸By faith Abraham obeyed when he was called to go out to the place which he would receive as an inheritance. And he went out, not knowing where he was going. ⁹By faith he dwelt in the land of promise as *in* a foreign country, dwelling in tents with Isaac and Jacob, the heirs with him of the same promise; ¹⁰for he waited for the city which has foundations, whose builder and maker *is* God. ¹¹By faith Sarah herself also received strength to conceive seed, and she bore a child when she was past the age, because she judged Him faithful who had promised. ¹²Therefore from one man, and him as good as dead, were born *as many* as the stars of the sky in multitude—innumerable as the sand which is by the seashore. ¹³These all died in faith, not having received the promises, but having seen them afar off were assured of them, embraced *them* and confessed that they were strangers and pilgrims on the earth.

What insight does God give us in this Scripture about the characteristics of a Christ-centered marriage?

What distractions are noted in this text that might tempt someone to not embrace characteristics of a Christ-centered marriage?

Take a minute and ask the Lord how He wants you to apply this Scripture to your life going forward (and we'll go around the room)?

#38   Hebrews 10:19-31 (WEB)

Having therefore, brothers, boldness to enter into the holy place by the blood of Jesus, 20 by the way which he dedicated for us, a new and living way, through the veil, that is to say, his flesh, 21 and having a great priest over God's house, 22 let's draw near with a true heart in fullness of faith, having our hearts sprinkled from an evil conscience, and having our body washed with pure water, 23 let's hold fast the confession of our hope without wavering; for he who promised is faithful. 24 Let's consider how to provoke one another to love and good works, 25 not forsaking our own assembling together, as the custom of some is, but exhorting one another, and so much the more as you see the Day approaching. 26 For if we sin willfully after we have received the knowledge of the truth, there remains no more a sacrifice for sins, 27 but a certain fearful expectation of judgment, and a fierceness of fire which will devour the adversaries. 28 A man who disregards Moses' law dies without compassion on the word of two or three witnesses. 29 How much worse punishment do you think he will be judged worthy of who has trodden under foot the Son of God, and has counted the blood of the covenant with which he was sanctified an unholy thing, and has insulted the Spirit of grace? 30 For we know him who said, "Vengeance belongs to me. I will repay," says the Lord. Deuteronomy 32:35 Again, "The Lord will judge his people." Deuteronomy 32:36; Psalm 135:14 31 It is a fearful thing to fall into the hands of the living God.

What insight does God give us in this Scripture about the characteristics of a Christ-centered marriage?

What distractions are noted in this text that might tempt someone to not embrace characteristics of a Christ-centered marriage?

Take a minute and ask the Lord how He wants you to apply this Scripture to your life going forward (and we'll go around the room)?

#39 Galatians 6:1-10 (WEB)

Brothers, even if a man is caught in some fault, you who are spiritual must restore such a one in a spirit of gentleness; looking to yourself so that you also aren't tempted. ²Bear one another's burdens, and so fulfill the law of Christ. ³For if a man thinks himself to be something when he is nothing, he deceives himself. ⁴But let each man examine his own work, and then he will have reason to boast in himself, and not in someone else. ⁵For each man will bear his own burden. ⁶But let him who is taught in the word share all good things with him who teaches. ⁷Don't be deceived. God is not mocked, for whatever a man sows, that he will also reap. ⁸For he who sows to his own flesh will from the flesh reap corruption. But he who sows to the Spirit will from the Spirit reap eternal life. ⁹Let's not be weary in doing good, for we will reap in due season, if we don't give up. ¹⁰So then, as we have opportunity, let's do what is good toward all men, and especially toward those who are of the household of the faith.

What insight does God give us in this Scripture about the characteristics of a Christ-centered marriage?

What distractions are noted in this text that might tempt someone to not embrace characteristics of a Christ-centered marriage?

Take a minute and ask the Lord how He wants you to apply this Scripture to your life going forward (and we'll go around the room)?

Communication and Forgiveness
#40   Ephesians 4:25-32 (WEB)

Therefore putting away falsehood, speak truth each one with his neighbor. For we are members of one another. ²⁶ "Be angry, and don't sin." Psalm 4:4 Don't let the sun go down on your wrath, ²⁷ and don't give place to the devil. ²⁸ Let him who stole steal no more; but rather let him labor, producing with his hands something that is good, that he may have something to give to him who has need. ²⁹ Let no corrupt speech proceed out of your mouth, but only what is good for building others up as the need may be, that it may give grace to those who hear. ³⁰ Don't grieve the Holy Spirit of God, in whom you were sealed for the day of redemption. ³¹ Let all bitterness, wrath, anger, outcry, and slander be put away from you, with all malice. ³² And be kind to one another, tender hearted, forgiving each other, just as God also in Christ forgave you.

What insight does God give us in this Scripture about the characteristics of a Christ-centered marriage?

What distractions are noted in this text that might tempt someone to not embrace characteristics of a Christ-centered marriage?

Take a minute and ask the Lord how He wants you to apply this Scripture to your life going forward (and we'll go around the room)?

#41   Matthew 6:9-21 (WEB)

Pray like this: "'Our Father in heaven, may your name be kept holy. [10] Let your Kingdom come. Let your will be done on earth as it is in heaven. [11] Give us today our daily bread. [12] Forgive us our debts, as we also forgive our debtors. [13] Bring us not into temptation, but deliver us from the evil one. For yours is the Kingdom, the power, and the glory forever. Amen.' [14] "For if you forgive men their trespasses, your heavenly Father will also forgive you. [15] But if you don't forgive men their trespasses, neither will your Father forgive your trespasses. [16] "Moreover when you fast, don't be like the hypocrites, with sad faces. For they disfigure their faces that they may be seen by men to be fasting. Most certainly I tell you, they have received their reward. [17] But you, when you fast, anoint your head and wash your face, [18] so that you are not seen by men to be fasting, but by your Father who is in secret; and your Father, who sees in secret, will reward you. [19] "Don't lay up treasures for yourselves on the earth, where moth and rust consume, and where thieves break through and steal; [20] but lay up for yourselves treasures in heaven, where neither moth nor rust consume, and where thieves don't break through and steal; [21] for where your treasure is, there your heart will be also.

What insight does God give us in this Scripture about the characteristics of a Christ-centered marriage?

What distractions are noted in this text that might tempt someone to not embrace characteristics of a Christ-centered marriage?

Take a minute and ask the Lord how He wants you to apply this Scripture to your life going forward (and we'll go around the room)?

#42   Mark 11:22-33 (AMPC)

And Jesus, replying, said to them, Have faith in God [constantly]. ²³ Truly I tell you, whoever says to this mountain, Be lifted up and thrown into the sea! and does not doubt at all in his heart but believes that what he says will take place, it will be done for him. ²⁴ For this reason I am telling you, whatever you ask for in prayer, believe (trust and be confident) that it is granted to you, and you will [get it]. ²⁵ And whenever you stand praying, if you have anything against anyone, forgive him *and* let it drop (leave it, let it go), in order that your Father Who is in heaven may also forgive you your [own] failings *and* shortcomings *and* let them drop. ²⁶ *But if you do not forgive, neither will your Father in heaven forgive your failings and shortcomings.* ²⁷ And they came again to Jerusalem. And when Jesus was walking about in the courts and porches of the] temple, the chief priests and the scribes and the elders came to Him, ²⁸ And they kept saying to Him, By what [sort of] authority are You doing these things, or who gave You this authority to do them? ²⁹ Jesus told them, I will ask you a question. Answer Me, and then I will tell you by what [sort of] authority I do these things. ³⁰ Was the baptism of John from heaven or from men? Answer Me. ³¹ And they reasoned *and* argued with one another, If we say, From heaven, He will say, Why then did you not believe him? ³² But [on the other hand] can we say, From men? For they were afraid of the people, because everybody considered *and* held John actually to be a prophet. ³³ So they replied to Jesus, We do not know. And Jesus said to them, Neither am I going to tell you what [sort of] authority I have for doing these things.

What insight does God give us in this Scripture about the characteristics of a Christ-centered marriage?

What distractions are noted in this text that might tempt someone to not embrace characteristics of a Christ-centered marriage?

Take a minute and ask the Lord how He wants you to apply this Scripture to your life going forward (and we'll go around the room)?

#43   Luke 17:1-10 (WEB)

He said to the disciples, "It is impossible that no occasions of stumbling should come, but woe to him through whom they come! ² It would be better for him if a millstone were hung around his neck, and he were thrown into the sea, rather than that he should cause one of these little ones to stumble. ³ Be careful. If your brother sins against you, rebuke him. If he repents, forgive him. ⁴ If he sins against you seven times in the day, and seven times returns, saying, 'I repent,' you shall forgive him." ⁵ The apostles said to the Lord, "Increase our faith." ⁶ The Lord said, "If you had faith like a grain of mustard seed, you would tell this sycamore tree, 'Be uprooted, and be planted in the sea,' and it would obey you. ⁷ But who is there among you, having a servant plowing or keeping sheep, that will say when he comes in from the field, 'Come immediately and sit down at the table,' ⁸ and will not rather tell him, 'Prepare my supper, clothe yourself properly, and serve me, while I eat and drink. Afterward you shall eat and drink'? ⁹ Does he thank that servant because he did the things that were commanded? I think not. ¹⁰ Even so you also, when you have done all the things that are commanded you, say, 'We are unworthy servants. We have done our duty.'"

What insight does God give us in this Scripture about the characteristics of a Christ-centered marriage?

What distractions are noted in this text that might tempt someone to not embrace characteristics of a Christ-centered marriage?

Take a minute and ask the Lord how He wants you to apply this Scripture to your life going forward (and we'll go around the room)?

#44   Matthew 18:21-35 (WEB)

Then Peter came and said to him, "Lord, how often shall my brother sin against me, and I forgive him? Until seven times?" 22 Jesus said to him, "I don't tell you until seven times, but, until seventy times seven. 23 Therefore the Kingdom of Heaven is like a certain king, who wanted to settle accounts with his servants. 24 When he had begun to settle, one was brought to him who owed him ten thousand talents. 25 But because he couldn't pay, his lord commanded him to be sold, with his wife, his children, and all that he had, and payment to be made. 26 The servant therefore fell down and knelt before him, saying, 'Lord, have patience with me, and I will repay you all!' 27 The lord of that servant, being moved with compassion, released him and forgave him the debt. 28 "But that servant went out and found one of his fellow servants who owed him one hundred denarii, and he grabbed him and took him by the throat, saying, 'Pay me what you owe!' 29 "So his fellow servant fell down at his feet and begged him, saying, 'Have patience with me, and I will repay you!' 30 He would not, but went and cast him into prison until he should pay back that which was due. 31 So when his fellow servants saw what was done, they were exceedingly sorry, and came and told their lord all that was done. 32 Then his lord called him in and said to him, 'You wicked servant! I forgave you all that debt because you begged me. 33 Shouldn't you also have had mercy on your fellow servant, even as I had mercy on you?' 34 His lord was angry, and delivered him to the tormentors until he should pay all that was due to him. 35 So my heavenly Father will also do to you, if you don't each forgive your brother from your hearts for his misdeeds."

What insight does God give us in this Scripture about the characteristics of a Christ-centered marriage?

What distractions are noted in this text that might tempt someone to not embrace characteristics of a Christ-centered marriage?

Take a minute and ask the Lord how He wants you to apply this Scripture to your life going forward (and we'll go around the room)?

Patience and Appreciating One Another
#45   Ephesians 3:14-4:7 (WEB)

For this cause, I bow my knees to the Father of our Lord Jesus Christ, [15] from whom every family in heaven and on earth is named, [16] that he would grant you, according to the riches of his glory, that you may be strengthened with power through his Spirit in the inner person, [17] that Christ may dwell in your hearts through faith, to the end that you, being rooted and grounded in love, [18] may be strengthened to comprehend with all the saints what is the width and length and height and depth, [19] and to know Christ's love which surpasses knowledge, that you may be filled with all the fullness of God. [20] Now to him who is able to do exceedingly abundantly above all that we ask or think, according to the power that works in us, [21] to him be the glory in the assembly and in Christ Jesus to all generations forever and ever. Amen. I therefore, the prisoner in the Lord, beg you to walk worthily of the calling with which you were called, [2] with all lowliness and humility, with patience, bearing with one another in love, [3] being eager to keep the unity of the Spirit in the bond of peace. [4] There is one body and one Spirit, even as you also were called in one hope of your calling, [5] one Lord, one faith, one baptism, [6] one God and Father of all, who is over all and through all, and in us all. [7] But to each one of us, the grace was given according to the measure of the gift of Christ.

What insight does God give us in this Scripture about the characteristics of a Christ-centered marriage?

What distractions are noted in this text that might tempt someone to not embrace characteristics of a Christ-centered marriage?

Take a minute and ask the Lord how He wants you to apply this Scripture to your life going forward (and we'll go around the room)?

#46   Ephesians 4:1-16 (WEB)

I therefore, the prisoner in the Lord, beg you to walk worthily of the calling with which you were called, ²with all lowliness and humility, with patience, bearing with one another in love, ³being eager to keep the unity of the Spirit in the bond of peace. ⁴There is one body and one Spirit, even as you also were called in one hope of your calling, ⁵one Lord, one faith, one baptism, ⁶one God and Father of all, who is over all and through all, and in us all. ⁷But to each one of us, the grace was given according to the measure of the gift of Christ. ⁸Therefore he says, "When he ascended on high, he led captivity captive, and gave gifts to people." Psalm 68:18 ⁹Now this, "He ascended", what is it but that he also first descended into the lower parts of the earth? ¹⁰He who descended is the one who also ascended far above all the heavens, that he might fill all things. ¹¹He gave some to be apostles; and some, prophets; and some, evangelists; and some, shepherds and teachers; ¹²for the perfecting of the saints, to the work of serving, to the building up of the body of Christ, ¹³until we all attain to the unity of the faith and of the knowledge of the Son of God, to a full grown man, to the measure of the stature of the fullness of Christ, ¹⁴that we may no longer be children, tossed back and forth and carried about with every wind of doctrine, by the trickery of men, in craftiness, after the wiles of error; ¹⁵but speaking truth in love, we may grow up in all things into him who is the head, Christ, ¹⁶from whom all the body, being fitted and knit together through that which every joint supplies, according to the working in measure of each individual part, makes the body increase to the building up of itself in love.

What insight does God give us in this Scripture about the characteristics of a Christ-centered marriage?

What distractions are noted in this text that might tempt someone to not embrace characteristics of a Christ-centered marriage?

Take a minute and ask the Lord how He wants you to apply this Scripture to your life going forward (and we'll go around the room)?

#47 Ecclesiastes 4 (AMPC)

Then I returned and considered all the oppressions that are practiced under the sun: And I beheld the tears of the oppressed, and they had no comforter; and on the side of their oppressors was power, but they [too] had no comforter. ²So I praised *and* thought more fortunate those who have been long dead than the living, who are still alive. ³But better than them both [I thought] is he who has not yet been born, who has not seen the evil deeds that are done under the sun. ⁴Then I saw that all painful effort in labor and all skill in work comes from man's rivalry with his neighbor. This is also vanity, a vain striving after the wind *and* a feeding on it. ⁵The fool folds his hands together and eats his own flesh [destroying himself by indolence]. ⁶Better is a handful with quietness than both hands full with painful effort, a vain striving after the wind *and* a feeding on it. ⁷Then I returned, and I saw vanity under the sun [in one of its peculiar forms]. ⁸Here is one alone—no one with him; he neither has child nor brother. Yet there is no end to all his labor, neither is his eye satisfied with riches, neither does he ask, For whom do I labor and deprive myself of good? This is also vanity (emptiness, falsity, and futility); yes, it is a painful effort *and* an unhappy business. ⁹Two are better than one, because they have a good [more satisfying] reward for their labor; ¹⁰For if they fall, the one will lift up his fellow. But woe to him who is alone when he falls and has not another to lift him up! ¹¹Again, if two lie down together, then they have warmth; but how can one be warm alone? ¹²And though a man might prevail against him who is alone, two will withstand him. A threefold cord is not quickly broken. ¹³Better is a poor and wise youth than an old and foolish king who no longer knows how to receive counsel (friendly reproof and warning)— ¹⁴Even though [the youth] comes out of prison to reign, while the other, born a king, becomes needy. ¹⁵I saw all the living who walk under the sun with the youth who was to stand up in the king's stead. ¹⁶There was no end to all the people; he was over all of them.

Yet those who come later will not rejoice in him. Surely this also is vanity (emptiness, falsity, vainglory) and a striving after the wind *and a feeding on it*.

What insight does God give us in this Scripture about the characteristics of a Christ-centered marriage?

What distractions are noted in this text that might tempt someone to not embrace characteristics of a Christ-centered marriage?

Take a minute and ask the Lord how He wants you to apply this Scripture to your life going forward (and we'll go around the room)?

#48 Ephesians 5:15-24 (WEB)

Therefore watch carefully how you walk, not as unwise, but as wise, ¹⁶ redeeming the time, because the days are evil. ¹⁷ Therefore don't be foolish, but understand what the will of the Lord is. ¹⁸ Don't be drunken with wine, in which is dissipation, but be filled with the Spirit, ¹⁹ speaking to one another in psalms, hymns, and spiritual songs; singing and making melody in your heart to the Lord; ²⁰ giving thanks always concerning all things in the name of our Lord Jesus Christ, to God, even the Father; ²¹ subjecting yourselves to one another in the fear of Christ. Wives, be subject to your own husbands, as to the Lord. ²³ For the husband is the head of the wife, as Christ also is the head of the assembly, being himself the Savior of the body. ²⁴ But as the assembly is subject to Christ, so let the wives also be to their own husbands in everything.

What insight does God give us in this Scripture about the characteristics of a Christ-centered marriage?

What distractions are noted in this text that might tempt someone to not embrace characteristics of a Christ-centered marriage?

Take a minute and ask the Lord how He wants you to apply this Scripture to your life going forward (and we'll go around the room)?

#49 Galatians 5:18-26 (NKJV)

But if you are led by the Spirit, you are not under the law. [19] Now the works of the flesh are evident, which are: adultery, fornication, uncleanness, lewdness, [20] idolatry, sorcery, hatred, contentions, jealousies, outbursts of wrath, selfish ambitions, dissensions, heresies, [21] envy, murders, drunkenness, revelries, and the like; of which I tell you beforehand, just as I also told *you* in time past, that those who practice such things will not inherit the kingdom of God. [22] But the fruit of the Spirit is love, joy, peace, longsuffering, kindness, goodness, faithfulness, [23] gentleness, self-control. Against such there is no law. [24] And those *who are* Christ's have crucified the flesh with its passions and desires. [25] If we live in the Spirit, let us also walk in the Spirit. [26] Let us not become conceited, provoking one another, envying one another.

What insight does God give us in this Scripture about the characteristics of a Christ-centered marriage?

What distractions are noted in this text that might tempt someone to not embrace characteristics of a Christ-centered marriage?

Take a minute and ask the Lord how He wants you to apply this Scripture to your life going forward (and we'll go around the room)?

Work/Life Balance
#50   1 Corinthians 6:9-20 (ESV)

Or do you not know that the unrighteous will not inherit the kingdom of God? Do not be deceived: neither the sexually immoral, nor idolaters, nor adulterers, nor men who practice homosexuality, [10] nor thieves, nor the greedy, nor drunkards, nor revilers, nor swindlers will inherit the kingdom of God. [11] And such were some of you. But you were washed, you were sanctified, you were justified in the name of the Lord Jesus Christ and by the Spirit of our God. [12] "All things are lawful for me," but not all things are helpful. "All things are lawful for me," but I will not be dominated by anything. [13] "Food is meant for the stomach and the stomach for food"—and God will destroy both one and the other. The body is not meant for sexual immorality, but for the Lord, and the Lord for the body. [14] And God raised the Lord and will also raise us up by his power. [15] Do you not know that your bodies are members of Christ? Shall I then take the members of Christ and make them members of a prostitute? Never! [16] Or do you not know that he who is joined to a prostitute becomes one body with her? For, as it is written, "The two will become one flesh." [17] But he who is joined to the Lord becomes one spirit with him. [18] Flee from sexual immorality. Every other sin a person commits is outside the body, but the sexually immoral person sins against his own body. [19] Or do you not know that your body is a temple of the Holy Spirit within you, whom you have from God? You are not your own, [20] for you were bought with a price. So glorify God in your body.

What insight does God give us in this Scripture about the characteristics of a Christ-centered marriage?

What distractions are noted in this text that might tempt someone to not embrace characteristics of a Christ-centered marriage?

Take a minute and ask the Lord how He wants you to apply this Scripture to your life going forward (and we'll go around the room)?

#51 1 Timothy 6:17-21 (WEB)

Charge those who are rich in this present world that they not be arrogant, nor have their hope set on the uncertainty of riches, but on the living God, who richly provides us with everything to enjoy; [18] that they do good, that they be rich in good works, that they be ready to distribute, willing to share; [19] laying up in store for themselves a good foundation against the time to come, that they may lay hold of eternal life. [20] Timothy, guard that which is committed to you, turning away from the empty chatter and oppositions of what is falsely called knowledge, [21] which some profess, and thus have wandered from the faith. Grace be with you. Amen.

What insight does God give us in this Scripture about the characteristics of a Christ-centered marriage?

What distractions are noted in this text that might tempt someone to not embrace characteristics of a Christ-centered marriage?

Take a minute and ask the Lord how He wants you to apply this Scripture to your life going forward (and we'll go around the room)?

#52 Matthew 26:36-41 (WEB)

Then Jesus came with them to a place called Gethsemane, and said to his disciples, "Sit here, while I go there and pray." ³⁷ He took with him Peter and the two sons of Zebedee, and began to be sorrowful and severely troubled. ³⁸ Then he said to them, "My soul is exceedingly sorrowful, even to death. Stay here and watch with me." ³⁹ He went forward a little, fell on his face, and prayed, saying, "My Father, if it is possible, let this cup pass away from me; nevertheless, not what I desire, but what you desire." ⁴⁰ He came to the disciples and found them sleeping, and said to Peter, "What, couldn't you watch with me for one hour? ⁴¹ Watch and pray, that you don't enter into temptation. The spirit indeed is willing, but the flesh is weak."

What insight does God give us in this Scripture about the characteristics of a Christ-centered marriage?

What distractions are noted in this text that might tempt someone to not embrace characteristics of a Christ-centered marriage?

Take a minute and ask the Lord how He wants you to apply this Scripture to your life going forward (and we'll go around the room)?

#53 Ephesians 5:1-13 (WEB)

Be therefore imitators of God, as beloved children. ²Walk in love, even as Christ also loved us and gave himself up for us, an offering and a sacrifice to God for a sweet-smelling fragrance. ³But sexual immorality, and all uncleanness or covetousness, let it not even be mentioned among you, as becomes saints; ⁴nor filthiness, nor foolish talking, nor jesting, which are not appropriate, but rather giving of thanks. ⁵Know this for sure, that no sexually immoral person, nor unclean person, nor covetous man, who is an idolater, has any inheritance in the Kingdom of Christ and God. ⁶Let no one deceive you with empty words. For because of these things, the wrath of God comes on the children of disobedience. ⁷Therefore don't be partakers with them. ⁸For you were once darkness, but are now light in the Lord. Walk as children of light, ⁹for the fruit of the Spirit is in all goodness and righteousness and truth, ¹⁰proving what is well pleasing to the Lord. ¹¹Have no fellowship with the unfruitful deeds of darkness, but rather even reprove them. ¹²For it is a shame even to speak of the things which are done by them in secret. ¹³But all things, when they are reproved, are revealed by the light, for everything that reveals is light.

What insight does God give us in this Scripture about the characteristics of a Christ-centered marriage?

What distractions are noted in this text that might tempt someone to not embrace characteristics of a Christ-centered marriage?

Take a minute and ask the Lord how He wants you to apply this Scripture to your life going forward (and we'll go around the room)?

#54   1 Corinthians 10:1-13 (WEB)

Now I would not have you ignorant, brothers, that our fathers were all under the cloud, and all passed through the sea; ²and were all baptized into Moses in the cloud and in the sea; ³and all ate the same spiritual food; ⁴and all drank the same spiritual drink. For they drank of a spiritual rock that followed them, and the rock was Christ. ⁵However with most of them, God was not well pleased, for they were overthrown in the wilderness. ⁶Now these things were our examples, to the intent we should not lust after evil things, as they also lusted. ⁷Don't be idolaters, as some of them were. As it is written, "The people sat down to eat and drink, and rose up to play." Exodus 32:6 ⁸Let's not commit sexual immorality, as some of them committed, and in one day twenty-three thousand fell. ⁹Let's not test Christ, as some of them tested, and perished by the serpents. ¹⁰Don't grumble, as some of them also grumbled, and perished by the destroyer. ¹¹Now all these things happened to them by way of example, and they were written for our admonition, on whom the ends of the ages have come. ¹²Therefore let him who thinks he stands be careful that he doesn't fall. ¹³No temptation has taken you except what is common to man. God is faithful, who will not allow you to be tempted above what you are able, but will with the temptation also make the way of escape, that you may be able to endure it.

What insight does God give us in this Scripture about the characteristics of a Christ-centered marriage?

Characteristics of a Great Christ-Centered Marriage

What distractions are noted in this text that might tempt someone to not embrace characteristics of a Christ-centered marriage?

Take a minute and ask the Lord how He wants you to apply this Scripture to your life going forward (and we'll go around the room)?

#55 1 Peter 5:8-14 (WEB)

Be sober and self-controlled. Be watchful. Your adversary, the devil, walks around like a roaring lion, seeking whom he may devour. ⁹Withstand him steadfast in your faith, knowing that your brothers who are in the world are undergoing the same sufferings. ¹⁰But may the God of all grace, who called you to his eternal glory by Christ Jesus, after you have suffered a little while, perfect, establish, strengthen, and settle you. ¹¹To him be the glory and the power forever and ever. Amen. ¹²Through Silvanus, our faithful brother, as I consider him, I have written to you briefly, exhorting, and testifying that this is the true grace of God in which you stand. ¹³She who is in Babylon, chosen together with you, greets you. So does Mark, my son. ¹⁴Greet one another with a kiss of love. Peace be to all of you who are in Christ Jesus. Amen.

What insight does God give us in this Scripture about the characteristics of a Christ-centered marriage?

What distractions are noted in this text that might tempt someone to not embrace characteristics of a Christ-centered marriage?

Take a minute and ask the Lord how He wants you to apply this Scripture to your life going forward (and we'll go around the room)?

Investing in Your Children
#56   Ephesians 6:1-9 ^(WEB)

Children, obey your parents in the Lord, for this is right. ² "Honor your father and mother," which is the first commandment with a promise: ³ "that it may be well with you, and you may live long on the earth." Deuteronomy 5:16 ⁴ You fathers, don't provoke your children to wrath, but nurture them in the discipline and instruction of the Lord. ⁵ Servants, be obedient to those who according to the flesh are your masters, with fear and trembling, in singleness of your heart, as to Christ, ⁶ not in the way of service only when eyes are on you, as men pleasers, but as servants of Christ, doing the will of God from the heart, ⁷ with good will doing service as to the Lord, and not to men, ⁸ knowing that whatever good thing each one does, he will receive the same good again from the Lord, whether he is bound or free. ⁹ You masters, do the same things to them, and give up threatening, knowing that he who is both their Master and yours is in heaven, and there is no partiality with him.

What insight does God give us in this Scripture about the characteristics of a Christ-centered marriage?

What distractions are noted in this text that might tempt someone to not embrace characteristics of a Christ-centered marriage?

Take a minute and ask the Lord how He wants you to apply this Scripture to your life going forward (and we'll go around the room)?

#57　Proverbs 22:1-16 (WEB)

A good name is more desirable than great riches, and loving favor is better than silver and gold. ²The rich and the poor have this in common: Yahweh is the maker of them all. ³A prudent man sees danger and hides himself; but the simple pass on, and suffer for it. ⁴The result of humility and the fear of Yahweh is wealth, honor, and life. ⁵Thorns and snares are in the path of the wicked: whoever guards his soul stays from them. ⁶Train up a child in the way he should go, and when he is old he will not depart from it. ⁷The rich rule over the poor. The borrower is servant to the lender. ⁸He who sows wickedness reaps trouble, and the rod of his fury will be destroyed. ⁹He who has a generous eye will be blessed; for he shares his food with the poor. ¹⁰Drive out the mocker, and strife will go out; yes, quarrels and insults will stop. ¹¹He who loves purity of heart and speaks gracefully is the king's friend. ¹²Yahweh's eyes watch over knowledge; but he frustrates the words of the unfaithful. ¹³The sluggard says, "There is a lion outside! I will be killed in the streets!" ¹⁴The mouth of an adulteress is a deep pit. He who is under Yahweh's wrath will fall into it. ¹⁵Folly is bound up in the heart of a child: the rod of discipline drives it far from him. ¹⁶Whoever oppresses the poor for his own increase and whoever gives to the rich, both come to poverty.

What insight does God give us in this Scripture about the characteristics of a Christ-centered marriage?

What distractions are noted in this text that might tempt someone to not embrace characteristics of a Christ-centered marriage?

Take a minute and ask the Lord how He wants you to apply this Scripture to your life going forward (and we'll go around the room)?

#58 Deuteronomy 6:1-9 (WEB)

Now these are the commandments, the statutes, and the ordinances, which Yahweh your God commanded to teach you, that you might do them in the land that you go over to possess; ²that you might fear Yahweh your God, to keep all his statutes and his commandments, which I command you—you, your son, and your son's son, all the days of your life; and that your days may be prolonged. ³Hear therefore, Israel, and observe to do it, that it may be well with you, and that you may increase mightily, as Yahweh, the God of your fathers, has promised to you, in a land flowing with milk and honey. ⁴Hear, Israel: Yahweh is our God. Yahweh is one. ⁵You shall love Yahweh your God with all your heart, with all your soul, and with all your might. ⁶These words, which I command you today, shall be on your heart; ⁷and you shall teach them diligently to your children, and shall talk of them when you sit in your house, and when you walk by the way, and when you lie down, and when you rise up. ⁸You shall bind them for a sign on your hand, and they shall be for frontlets between your eyes. ⁹You shall write them on the door posts of your house and on your gates.

What insight does God give us in this Scripture about the characteristics of a Christ-centered marriage?

What distractions are noted in this text that might tempt someone to not embrace characteristics of a Christ-centered marriage?

Take a minute and ask the Lord how He wants you to apply this Scripture to your life going forward (and we'll go around the room)?

#59   Colossians 3:18-4:6 (NKJV)

Wives, submit to your own husbands, as is fitting in the Lord. [19] Husbands, love your wives and do not be bitter toward them. [20] Children, obey your parents in all things, for this is well pleasing to the Lord. [21] Fathers, do not provoke your children, lest they become discouraged. [22] Bondservants, obey in all things your masters according to the flesh, not with eyeservice, as men-pleasers, but in sincerity of heart, fearing God. [23] And whatever you do, do it heartily, as to the Lord and not to men, [24] knowing that from the Lord you will receive the reward of the inheritance; for you serve the Lord Christ. [25] But he who does wrong will be repaid for what he has done, and there is no partiality. [4:1] Masters, give your bondservants what is just and fair, knowing that you also have a Master in heaven. [2] Continue earnestly in prayer, being vigilant in it with thanksgiving; [3] meanwhile praying also for us, that God would open to us a door for the word, to speak the mystery of Christ, for which I am also in chains, [4] that I may make it manifest, as I ought to speak. [5] Walk in wisdom toward those *who are* outside, redeeming the time. [6] *Let* your speech always *be* with grace, seasoned with salt, that you may know how you ought to answer each one.

What insight does God give us in this Scripture about the characteristics of a Christ-centered marriage?

What distractions are noted in this text that might tempt someone to not embrace characteristics of a Christ-centered marriage?

Take a minute and ask the Lord how He wants you to apply this Scripture to your life going forward (and we'll go around the room)?

Joy and Hope for the Future
#60   Proverbs 17:16-28 (WEB)

Why is there money in the hand of a fool to buy wisdom, since he has no understanding? [17] A friend loves at all times; and a brother is born for adversity. [18] A man void of understanding strikes hands, and becomes collateral in the presence of his neighbor. [19] He who loves disobedience loves strife. One who builds a high gate seeks destruction. [20] One who has a perverse heart doesn't find prosperity, and one who has a deceitful tongue falls into trouble. [21] He who becomes the father of a fool grieves. The father of a fool has no joy. [22] A cheerful heart makes good medicine, but a crushed spirit dries up the bones. [23] A wicked man receives a bribe in secret, to pervert the ways of justice. [24] Wisdom is before the face of one who has understanding, but the eyes of a fool wander to the ends of the earth. [25] A foolish son brings grief to his father, and bitterness to her who bore him. [26] Also to punish the righteous is not good, nor to flog officials for their integrity. [27] He who spares his words has knowledge. He who is even tempered is a man of understanding. [28] Even a fool, when he keeps silent, is counted wise. When he shuts his lips, he is thought to be discerning.

What insight does God give us in this Scripture about the characteristics of a Christ-centered marriage?

What distractions are noted in this text that might tempt someone to not embrace characteristics of a Christ-centered marriage?

Take a minute and ask the Lord how He wants you to apply this Scripture to your life going forward (and we'll go around the room)?

#61 Romans 15:1-13 (WEB)

Now we who are strong ought to bear the weaknesses of the weak, and not to please ourselves. ²Let each one of us please his neighbor for that which is good, to be building him up. ³For even Christ didn't please himself. But, as it is written, "The reproaches of those who reproached you fell on me." Psalm 69:9 ⁴For whatever things were written before were written for our learning, that through perseverance and through encouragement of the Scriptures we might have hope. ⁵Now the God of perseverance and of encouragement grant you to be of the same mind with one another according to Christ Jesus, ⁶that with one accord you may with one mouth glorify the God and Father of our Lord Jesus Christ. ⁷Therefore accept one another, even as Christ also accepted you, to the glory of God. ⁸Now I say that Christ has been made a servant of the circumcision for the truth of God, that he might confirm the promises given to the fathers, ⁹and that the Gentiles might glorify God for his mercy. As it is written, "Therefore I will give praise to you among the Gentiles and sing to your name." 2 Samuel 22:50; Psalm 18:49 ¹⁰Again he says, "Rejoice, you Gentiles, with his people." Deuteronomy 32:43 ¹¹Again, "Praise the Lord, all you Gentiles! Let all the peoples praise him." Psalm 117:1 ¹²Again, Isaiah says, "There will be the root of Jesse, he who arises to rule over the Gentiles; in him the Gentiles will hope." Isaiah 11:10 ¹³Now may the God of hope fill you with all joy and peace in believing, that you may abound in hope, in the power of the Holy Spirit.

What insight does God give us in this Scripture about the characteristics of a Christ-centered marriage?

What distractions are noted in this text that might tempt someone to not embrace characteristics of a Christ-centered marriage?

Take a minute and ask the Lord how He wants you to apply this Scripture to your life going forward (and we'll go around the room)?

#62   Philippians 1:1-14 (WEB)

Paul and Timothy, servants of Jesus Christ; To all the saints in Christ Jesus who are at Philippi, with the overseers and servants: ² Grace to you, and peace from God our Father and the Lord Jesus Christ. ³ I thank my God whenever I remember you, ⁴ always in every request of mine on behalf of you all, making my requests with joy, ⁵ for your partnership in furtherance of the Good News from the first day until now; ⁶ being confident of this very thing, that he who began a good work in you will complete it until the day of Jesus Christ. ⁷ It is even right for me to think this way on behalf of all of you, because I have you in my heart, because both in my bonds and in the defense and confirmation of the Good News, you all are partakers with me of grace. ⁸ For God is my witness, how I long after all of you in the tender mercies of Christ Jesus. ⁹ This I pray, that your love may abound yet more and more in knowledge and all discernment, ¹⁰ so that you may approve the things that are excellent, that you may be sincere and without offense to the day of Christ, ¹¹ being filled with the fruits of righteousness, which are through Jesus Christ, to the glory and praise of God. ¹² Now I desire to have you know, brothers, that the things which happened to me have turned out rather to the progress of the Good News, ¹³ so that it became evident to the whole palace guard, and to all the rest, that my bonds are in Christ, ¹⁴ and that most of the brothers in the Lord, being confident through my bonds, are more abundantly bold to speak the word of God without fear.

What insight does God give us in this Scripture about the characteristics of a Christ-centered marriage?

What distractions are noted in this text that might tempt someone to not embrace characteristics of a Christ-centered marriage?

Take a minute and ask the Lord how He wants you to apply this Scripture to your life going forward (and we'll go around the room)?

#63 Romans 8:24-34 (NASB1995)

For in hope we have been saved, but hope that is seen is not hope; for who hopes for what he *already* sees? [25] But if we hope for what we do not see, with perseverance we wait eagerly for it. [26] In the same way the Spirit also helps our weakness; for we do not know how to pray as we should, but the Spirit Himself intercedes for *us* with groanings too deep for words; [27] and He who searches the hearts knows what the mind of the Spirit is, because He intercedes for the saints according to *the will of* God. [28] And we know that God causes all things to work together for good to those who love God, to those who are called according to *His* purpose. [29] For those whom He foreknew, He also predestined *to become* conformed to the image of His Son, so that He would be the firstborn among many brethren; [30] and these whom He predestined, He also called; and these whom He called, He also justified; and these whom He justified, He also glorified. [31] What then shall we say to these things? If God *is* for us, who *is* against us? [32] He who did not spare His own Son, but delivered Him over for us all, how will He not also with Him freely give us all things? [33] Who will bring a charge against God's elect? God is the one who justifies; [34] who is the one who condemns? Christ Jesus is He who died, yes, rather who was raised, who is at the right hand of God, who also intercedes for us.

What insight does God give us in this Scripture about the characteristics of a Christ-centered marriage?

What distractions are noted in this text that might tempt someone to not embrace characteristics of a Christ-centered marriage?

Take a minute and ask the Lord how He wants you to apply this Scripture to your life going forward (and we'll go around the room)?

#64   Psalm 16 (NKJV)

Preserve me, O God, for in You I put my trust. ²*O my soul,* you have said to the Lord, "You *are* my Lord, my goodness is nothing apart from You." ³As for the saints who *are* on the earth, "They are the excellent ones, in whom is all my delight." ⁴Their sorrows shall be multiplied who hasten *after* another *god;* their drink offerings of blood I will not offer, nor take up their names on my lips. ⁵O Lord, *You are* the portion of my inheritance and my cup; You maintain my lot. ⁶The lines have fallen to me in pleasant *places;* yes, I have a good inheritance. ⁷I will bless the Lord who has given me counsel; my heart also instructs me in the night seasons. ⁸I have set the Lord always before me; because *He is* at my right hand I shall not be moved. ⁹Therefore my heart is glad, and my glory rejoices; my flesh also will rest in hope. ¹⁰For You will not leave my soul in Sheol, nor will You allow Your Holy One to see corruption. ¹¹You will show me the path of life; in Your presence *is* fullness of joy; at Your right hand *are* pleasures forevermore.

What insight does God give us in this Scripture about the characteristics of a Christ-centered marriage?

What distractions are noted in this text that might tempt someone to not embrace characteristics of a Christ-centered marriage?

Take a minute and ask the Lord how He wants you to apply this Scripture to your life going forward (and we'll go around the room)?

Appendix A – Instructor Guide for Interactive Bible Learning

A well-prepared Interactive Bible Learning (IBL) leader takes time to read and reflect on the questions before the meeting, documenting their own answers—not to "teach," but to create a more engaging and personal learning experience for everyone else.

The questions are designed to keep the group focused on the Bible passage being studied. Please try to avoid straying into unrelated philosophies, personal doctrines, or theological debates. This is more about *them* self-discovering a relationship with God through the Word of God (hear the Word). It's about *them* learning how to get understanding from the Holy Spirit who gives understanding; they will need His help to answer the questions. It's about *them* learning how to be doers of the Word. Your job is to keep the meeting focused on the Word. A well-run meeting is highly interactive, gentle, and full of love/truth. You will likely sense the presence and affirmation of the Holy Spirit, because the focus is on the Word, and the power is in the Word. And it should be fun learning together and watching one another grow.

Now, this may be hard for some, but leaders should resist the urge to *teach*. Instead, let it be about *them* learning. Let *them* process verbally; give *them* time to respond to the questions. If there are moments of silence, embrace them—it often means people are thinking, reflecting, or seeking the Holy Spirit's guidance. The goal is for *them* to self-discover the joy of reading, understanding, and doing the Word. This builds confidence in Christ. This lays a sure foundation which is the Word of God. And God does the increase.

Be more like an orchestra leader: keep the meeting moving along, keep it interactive, prefer others to self, and let them teach while you lead. One way to keep the meeting well balanced is to smile a lot, affirm responses, say "thank you" to show appreciation and love. If the conversation is going astray, repeat the question. Before moving onto the next question, always ask if anyone else has any thoughts about the question. Be encouraging, be gentle, be loving. Be patient with yourself and others throughout the learning process. Stay humble—sometimes you'll be teaching/leading, other times you will be learning/leading. Also, be aware that sometimes God anoints the least expected in the group to impact the life of someone else in the group, even better than you! That's not just okay—it's exciting. And God gets the glory!

The following is a typical meeting format...

1. **Open with Prayer**
   Begin the meeting with a prayer, inviting the Holy Spirit to lead the discussion and bring understanding.

2. **Ask someone to read**
   The facilitator invites a volunteer to read the Scripture passage aloud. This practice helps the group engage in both hearing and absorbing the Word.

3. **Read the first question**
   The leader reads the question first question, *"What insight does God give us in this Scripture about the topic we are studying?"*

4. **Orchestrate**
   The leader's job is to make sure everyone else is talking, interactive, learning, processing, edifying, building up, equipping, sharing. When someone is finished, thank them, ask if there is anyone else? Re-read the question if it's too silent or needs to be re-focused.

5. **Read the second question**
   The second question (in case someone asks) is a question to help us know our enemy, which are distractions of the flesh, sin, world, and devil that keep us from hearing the Word and doing it.

6. **Read the last question**
   The last question is, *"Take a minute and ask the Lord how He wants you to apply this Scripture to your life going forward (and we'll go around the room)?"* After you read the question let the room be silent for a minute. It's a challenging question, but so important. Help them learn how to not only read the Word but do it (builds house on the rock). Then go around the room and make sure everyone shares. If they're not sure how to answer it, the first two questions will help them answer. No one is hidden.

7. **Close in Prayer**
   End the session with prayer. You may ask for prayer requests.

We suggest you commit to praying for one another throughout the study too. And a really good IBL leader will

The Good News about Jesus Christ

Interactive Bible Learning leaders may become aware that someone in the group has not yet experienced the joy of repentance and salvation. Here is a concise gospel message and believers response to help guide that conversation.

1. **Who is Jesus Christ?**

Jesus Christ is the Son of God sent from heaven. He is the Messiah, the Christ, the Lamb of God, the only Son of God. He is *Immanuel*, meaning *"God with us."* He is the eternal Word of God—who was with God in the beginning, who was God, and who came to dwell among us.

Jesus was the only perfect, sinless person to ever walk the earth. He came from heaven to become the perfect sacrifice, required to cleanse us from sin and unbelief. He is the only way to God the Father and the only one who gives eternal life. He is the Lord and Savior who was prophesied about from the very beginning of time.

2. **What Did Jesus Do?**

Jesus paid the ultimate price for us. On the cross, He shed His blood—once and for all mankind. His blood was necessary because God designed forgiveness to come through the shedding of blood. Jesus was the perfect, sinless sacrifice who willingly died in our place.

But that's not the end of the story—He rose from the dead! Through His resurrection, He demonstrated His power over sin and death, opening the door to heaven. He declared, "I am the resurrection and the life"—for all who believe in Him.

Jesus reconciles us to God and gives us new life—eternal life. His sacrifice is a gift from God—one that we could never earn but is freely given because of His grace, mercy, forgiveness, and unfailing love. That is the Good News!

3. **Our response**

If someone is ready to take this step, encourage them to pray, confess their faith in Jesus, and embrace the new life He has given them. To receive the gift of salvation, we are encouraged to:

- Repent—turn to Jesus, turning away from sin.
- Believe—with all our heart, trust that He is who He says He is and that He has done what He said He has done.
- Confess—declare that Jesus is Lord over our lives.
- Receive—accept the forgiveness of sins and the gift of the Holy Spirit.

When we respond to the Good News—the gospel of Jesus Christ—we are saved and born again of the Holy Spirit. This is not something we achieve by our own efforts but a gift of grace received through faith in Jesus Christ. In Him, we are made new, transformed by His love and power.

4. **A Prayer of Salvation**

Perhaps you've known these truths in your mind—maybe through a religious background or reciting the Apostle's Creed—but now, it's time to believe in your heart.

- Are you ready to leave behind your old life and turn to Him?
- Are you ready to receive the gift of new life in Christ?
- Are you ready to be cleansed of all your sins
- Are you ready to receive the glorious gift of the Holy Spirit, who will dwell in you and guide you?
- Do you sense that God is drawing you to Himself?

If so, this is a beautiful moment—let's confess our faith in Jesus together. Repeat after me:

"Jesus (Jesus), I believe You are Immanuel—God with us (repeat)... I believe You came from Heaven... died on the cross for my sins... and that You were resurrected from the dead... I confess that I have sinned and fallen short... I turn to You now... I leave my old life behind... I need a Savior, and that Savior is You, Jesus... Please cleanse me of my sins... and all unrighteousness..."

[Pause for a moment—receive the forgiveness of sins.]

"Thank You for what You've done on the cross... Thank You for eternal life... Thank You for the gift of the Holy Spirit... I receive Your Holy Spirit in my heart now, in the name of Jesus..."

[Pause again—allow time to receive the Holy Spirit. If appropriate, this may also be a time for the laying on of hands in prayer.]

Now, let's take a moment and celebrate what the Lord has done! This is the beginning of a new life in Christ—one filled with His love, guidance, and presence. Welcome to the family of God!

www.ingramcontent.com/pod-product-compliance
Lightning Source LLC
Chambersburg PA
CBHW070502090426
42735CB00012B/2656